Healthy Lifestyles 2

The Complete Package for Junior Cycle SPHE

Catherine Deegan & Edel O'Brien

Gill Education
Hume Avenue
Park West
Dublin 12
www.gilleducation.ie

Gill Education is an imprint of M.H. Gill & Co.

Design by Tanya M Ross Elementinc.ie
Illustrations by Derry Dillon

The paper used in this book is made from the wood pulp of managed forests. For every tree felled, at least one tree is planted, thereby renewing natural resources.

Any links to external websites should not be construed as an endorsement by Gill Education of the content or view of the linked material. Furthermore it cannot be guaranteed that all external links will be live.

For permission to reproduce photographs, the authors and publisher gratefully acknowledge the following:

© Advertising Archive: 99R; © Alamy: 16B, 20T, 20B, 24, 31, 35, 43, 45, 65T, 99L, 108C, 112, 118, 120, 124T, 124C, 124B, 128, 131, 134T, 134CB, 134BT, 134B, 135T, 135B, 138, 140TL, 140CL, 140CR, 140BR, 143; © Science Photo Library: 105, 107, 108T; © Shutterstock: 1, 16T, 27, 50, 50, 57, 57, 62, 65C, 65CB, 65B, 66, 87, 106, 134TB, 134CT, 140BL, 140TR; Courtesy of Irish Water Safety (iws.ie): 75.

The authors and publisher have made every effort to trace all copyright holders, but if any has been inadvertently overlooked we would be pleased to make the necessary arrangement at the first opportunity.

Acknowledgements
The authors and publisher are grateful to the following for permission to reproduce copyrighted material:

Learning Style Quiz adapted from Special Education Support Service www.sess.ie

'Faced with the sober reality of a drunken night out with our teens' by Emma Blain, courtesy of the Sunday Independent.

The authors and publisher have made every effort to trace all copyright holders, but if any has been inadvertently overlooked we would be pleased to make the necessary arrangement at the first opportunity.

Contents

Preface iv

Topic 1 Self Management 01
Lesson 1 Looking Back, Looking Forward 02
Lesson 2 What Motivates Me? 08
Lesson 3 Study Skills 13
Lesson 4 Making Decisions 18

STRAND 1
Who am I?

Topic 2 My Rights and the Rights of Others 24
Lesson 5 Group Work 25
Lesson 6 Family Ties 29

STRAND 1
Who am I?

Topic 3 Respectful Communication 35
Lesson 7 Assertive Communication 36

STRAND 2
Minding Myself and Others

Topic 4 Having a Friend and Being a friend 43
Lesson 8 The Changing Nature of Friendship 44

STRAND 3
Team Up

Topic 5 Anti-bullying 50
Lesson 9 Cyberbullying 51
Lesson 10 Feeling Threatened and Staying Safe Online 56

STRAND 3
Team Up

Topic 6 Being Healthy 62
Lesson 11 Body Care and Body Image 63
Lesson 12 Feeling Unwell 68
Lesson 13 Water Safety 74
Lesson 14 Accidents at Home and at School 79

STRAND 2
Minding Myself and Others

Topic 7 Positive Mental Health 87
Lesson 15 Self-confidence 88
Lesson 16 Positive and Negative Influences 93
Lesson 17 Body Image 98

STRAND 4
Mental Health and Wellbeing

Topic 8 Sexuality and Sexual Health 104
Lesson 18 From Conception to Birth 105

STRAND 2
Minding Myself and Others

Topic 9 Relationship Spectrum 112
Lesson 19 Peer Pressure and Other Influences 113

STRAND 3
Team Up

Topic 10 Special Relationships 118
Lesson 20 Recognising and Expressing Feelings and Emotions 119
Lesson 21 Managing Relationships 123
Lesson 22 Health and Personal Safety 127

STRAND 3
Team Up

Topic 11 Substance Use 131
Lesson 23 The Effects of Drugs 132
Lesson 24 Alcohol and its Effects: Why/Why Not? 137
Lesson 25 Cannabis and its Effects: Why/Why Not? 142

STRAND 2
Minding Myself and Others

Preface

Welcome to *New Healthy Lifestyles*

This new edition retains all of the lessons required for teaching the existing modular course: simply follow the **Modular Course Overview** on page v to do so. It is also designed to fulfil the criteria for teaching SPHE as a **Short Course** for the new Junior Cycle: The contents list on page iii is structured around the topics and strands recommended for the new Short Course in SPHE.

The **Up for the Challenge** feature at the end of each topic allows students to apply what they have learned to real life situations. These challenges also prepare students for assessment related to the certification of the short course; see your **Teacher's Resource Book on gillexplore.ie** for more detail.

We have retained many of the favourite features of the highly popular first edition, such as crosswords and wordsearches. We have also added the following features, which means that, whatever approach your school is taking for SPHE, you will have an easy-to-follow and comprehensive set of lessons for your classes. These new features include:

- A ready-to-go, lesson-by-lesson approach
- A Teacher's Resource Book available on gillmacmillan.ie which gives practical guidelines on how to implement the material in the student books
- Links to websites which provide extra background information for the teacher and enhances the student's knowledge of a topic
- Each lesson is based on the experiential learning model which means that students will be actively engaged in their own learning
- Each lesson concludes with a **Learning Keepsake**, which ensures students maintain a personal learning journal as recommended by the NCCA.
- Exercises to improve students' literacy and numeracy skills are in-built
- An **eBook** version which contains many fun videos and animations to enhance lessons
- Extra lessons and exciting and interesting worksheets and articles in our Teacher's Resource Book.

New Healthy Lifestyles has received very positive reviews from SPHE teachers who have used it in class. They have found it fun, relevant and up to date and we hope you do too!

Edel O'Brien and Catherine Deegan

Modular Course Overview

Module 1 Belonging and Integrating   **Tick when completed**

Lesson 1 Looking Back, Looking Forward   2   ☐
Lesson 5 Group Work   25   ☐
Lesson 6 Family Ties   29   ☐

Module 2 Self Management: A Sense of Purpose

Lesson 2 What Motivates Me?   8   ☐
Lesson 3 Study Skills   13   ☐

Module 3 Communication Skills

Lesson 7 Assertive Communication   36   ☐

Module 4 Physical Health

Lesson 11 Body Care and Body Image   63   ☐
Lesson 12 Feeling Unwell   68   ☐

Module 5 Friendship

Lesson 8 The Changing Nature of Friendship   44   ☐
Lesson 9 Cyberbullying   51   ☐

Module 6 Relationships and Sexuality

Lesson 18 From Conception to Birth   105   ☐
Lesson 19 Peer Pressure and Other Influences   113   ☐
Lesson 20 Recognising and Expressing Feelings and Emotions   119   ☐
Lesson 21 Managing Relationships   123   ☐
Lesson 22 Health and Personal Safety   127   ☐

Module 7 Emotional Health

Lesson 15 Self-confidence   88   ☐
Lesson 17 Body Image   98   ☐

Module 8 Influences and Decisions

Lesson 4 Making Decisions   18   ☐
Lesson 16 Positive and Negative Influences   93   ☐

Module 9 Substance Abuse

Lesson 23 The Effects of Drugs   132   ☐
Lesson 24 Alcohol and its Effects: Why/Why Not?   137   ☐
Lesson 25 Cannabis and its Effects: Why/Why Not?   142   ☐

Module 10 Personal Safety

Lesson 10 Feeling Threatened and Staying Safe Online   56   ☐
Lesson 13 Water Safety   74   ☐
Lesson 14 Accidents at Home and at School   79   ☐

Self Management

- Lesson 1 Looking Back, Looking Forward
- Lesson 2 What Motivates Me?
- Lesson 3 Study Skills
- Lesson 4 Making Decisions

LESSON 1
Looking Back, Looking Forward

At the end of this lesson . . .
. . . you will have reviewed first year
. . . you will have identified your goals for second year.

Key Words
- Challenge
- Review

 # Keyskill
- Managing Myself

Looking Back, *Looking Forward*

Looking back on first year helps you to reflect on your achievements: it also helps you to make improvements in second year. Perhaps you would like to improve your report or maybe you would have liked to get involved in more extracurricular activities.

The start of second year is a great opportunity for you to set goals and make decisions about what you want to achieve in the year ahead. Fill in your personal review sheet on the next page.

First Year Review Sheet

Two highlights for me in first year were . . .

1. _____

2. _____

One of the biggest challenges for me in first year was . . .

_____

This year I'm looking forward to . . .

_____

My first year summer School Report

Subject	Grade	Comments

Subjects I could improve in:

_____

I will do this by:

_____

Other areas (e.g. hobbies, relationships, sports, family) I would like to improve on:

_____

I will do this by:

_____

In your review sheet you identified what went well in first year and what you would like to improve on for second year.

Based on the improvements you listed in your review sheet, set your goals, using the 'What, Why, When, Who and How' approach.

What do you want to achieve?

_____

Why do you want to achieve this?

_____

When do you want to achieve this?

_____

Who can help you achieve this?

_____

How can you get started?

_____

Individual Activity

Based on my review of first year, three things I would like to start, three things I would like to stop and three things I would like to continue are:

START

1. _____
2. _____
3. _____

STOP

1. _____
2. _____
3. _____

CONTINUE

1. _____
2. _____
3. _____

Learning *Keepsake*

Three things I have learned from reviewing first year are:

1. _____
2. _____
3. _____

As a result of what I have learned from reviewing first year, I will:

_____

_____

_____

_____ has shared this Learning Keepsake with me _____

Name of student   Parent's/guardian's signature

LESSON 2
What Motivates Me?

At the end of this lesson . . .
. . . you will have identified some of the people and supports in your life.

Key Words
- Motivation
- Encouragement

 # Keyskill
- Managing Myself

The story of the chicken
and the eagle

The story is told of a man who found an eagle's egg. He put it with his chicks and mother hens.

Soon the egg hatched. The young eagle grew up with all the other chickens. Whatever the chickens did, the eagle did too. He thought he was a chicken, just like them.

Since the chickens could only fly for a short distance, the eagle also learned to fly a short distance. He thought that was what he was supposed to do. So that was all that he thought he could do. And that was all he was able to do.

One day the eagle saw a bird flying high above him. He was very impressed. 'Who is that?' he asked the hens around him.

'That's the eagle, the king of the birds,' the hens told him. 'He belongs to the sky. We belong to the earth – we are chickens.'

So the eagle lived and died a chicken, for that's what he thought he was.

Individual Activity

1. Who did the eagle admire in this story?

_____

_____

2. Why was the eagle not motivated to fly like an eagle?

_____

_____

3. What is the message of the story?

_____

_____

_____

'You may never fly like an eagle, but you will have your own hopes and dreams.'
If you could achieve anything in life, what would it be and who could support you in achieving it?

_____

_____

_____

Class Activity

What motivates me?

As you can see, these individuals are motivated in different ways. Everyone needs motivation to achieve things in life. On the stairs below, write down what or who can help us to achieve what we want in life.

> My mother said she would give me €100 for every A I got in my summer exams so I am really going to study hard this year.

> I study hard at school because I want a career I enjoy and I want to have a good salary.

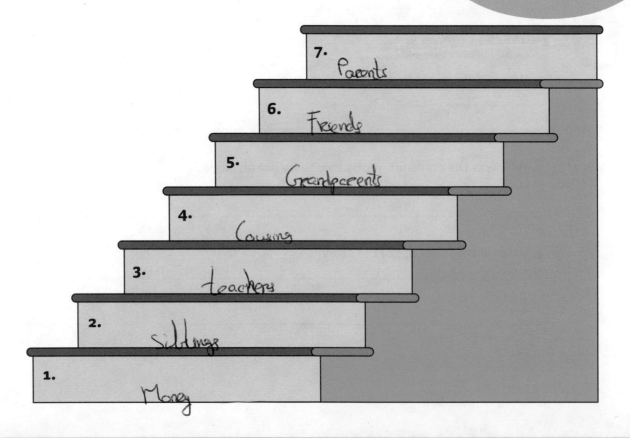

7. Parents

6. Friends

5. Grandparents

4. Cousins

3. Teachers

2. Siblings

1. Money

Now write down on the brick wall the people or things that can prevent or stop us achieving what we want.

Fogs

Ilness

drink

Lazyness

A bad
tein

Injuries

Bullies

Individual Activity

Imagine that in about ten years' time you are writing an autobiography in which you talk about your achievements. List three achievements that you are proud of.

1. Getting a ~~team~~
2. Getting a job
3. Getting a house

List three people or things that motivated you along the way.

1. The mother
2. The father
3. Friends

Learning *Keepsake*

Three things I have learned about what motivates me are:

1. Money _____
2. _____
3. _____

As a result of what I have learned about what motivates me, I will:

_____
_____
_____

_____ has shared this Learning Keepsake with me _____

Name of student   Parent's/guardian's signature

LESSON 3
Study Skills

At the end of this lesson . . .
. . . you will have identified your learning style

. . . you will have improved your study skills.

Key Words
- Visual
- Auditory
- Kinaesthetic
- Mnemonics

Keyskill
- Managing Myself

Learning *style quiz*

Complete the following quiz by ticking the appropriate column to discover your preferred learning style.

		Often	Some-times	Seldom/Never
1.	I can remember more about a subject from listening than from reading.			✓
2.	I follow written directions better than oral directions.		✓	
3.	I like to write things down or take notes.			✓
4.	I bear down extremely hard with pen or pencil when writing.		✓	
5.	I need explanations of diagrams, graphs or visual directions.			
6.	I enjoy working with tools.			✓
7.	I enjoy developing and making graphs and charts.			✓
8.	I can tell if two sounds match.		✓	
9.	I remember best by writing things down several times.			✓
10.	I can understand and follow directions better by using a map.			✓
11.	I do better at academic subjects by listening to lectures and tapes.			✓
12.	I play with coins and keys in my pockets.	✓		
13.	I find it easier to spell words by repeating the letters than by writing the word on paper.		✓	
14.	I can understand a news article better by reading about it in the paper than by hearing it on the radio.		✓	
15.	I chew gum or snack during studies.		✓	
16.	I feel the best way to remember a picture is in my head.			✓
17.	I learn spelling by finger spelling the words.			✓
18.	I would rather listen to a good lecture or speech than read about the same material.		✓	
19.	I am good at solving jigsaw puzzles and mazes.			✓
20.	I grip objects in my hand during learning periods.			✓
21.	I prefer listening to the news on the radio than reading a newspaper.		✓	

22.	I obtain information on an interesting subject by reading relevant materials.			
23.	I feel very comfortable touching others, hugging, shaking hands, etc.			
24.	I follow oral directions better than written ones.			

Now fill in the table from your answers above.

Award yourself 5 points for often, 3 points for sometimes and 1 point for seldom/never. Complete the grid by filling in the values and totalling each column.

Visual		Auditory		Kinaesthetic	
Question	Points	Question	Points	Question	Points
2.		1.		4.	
3.		5.		6.	
7.		8.		9.	
10.		11.		12.	
14.		13.		15.	
16.		18.		17.	
19.		21.		20.	
22.		24.		23.	
Total		Total		Total	

Source: adapted from *Learning Style Quiz* on *www.sess.ie*

Visual learners

These learners learn best when information is written down or presented in some other visual way, e.g. in a diagram, drawing or video.
If you are a visual learner, these study skills might help you.

1. Flash cards.
2. Highlighting, circling or underlining important words.
3. Using colour codes and charts to display information.
4. Studying in a quiet place.
5. Watching DVDs.
6. Taking notes and making lists.
7. Using mind maps.

Auditory learners

These learners learn best when they can listen to information, e.g. lectures, discussions and CDs.
If you are an auditory learner, these study skills might help you.

1. Reading aloud.
2. Discussing things with a study partner or your friends.
3. Giving oral reports.
4. Listening to CDs.
5. Participating in group study.
6. Repeating facts to yourself with your eyes closed.

Kinaesthetic learners

These learners learn best when they can physically get involved in what they are trying to learn. They usually excel at practical subjects.
If you are a kinaesthetic learner, the following study skills might help you.

1. Taking regular breaks from study.
2. Role plays.
3. Using mnemonics.
4. Using flash cards.
5. Practising making things.

Group Activity

Find the people in your class who have the same learning style as you. Based on your own experiences, discuss the study techniques that work for you. Design a PowerPoint presentation of these useful tips.

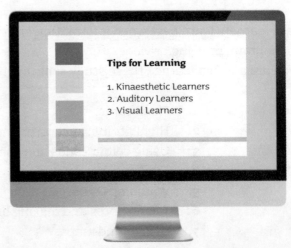

Tips for Learning

1. Kinaesthetic Learners
2. Auditory Learners
3. Visual Learners

Learning *Keepsake*

Three things I have discovered about my learning style are:

1. _____
2. _____
3. _____

As a result of what I have found out about my learning style, I will:

_____
_____
_____

_____ has shared this Learning Keepsake with me _____

Name of student   Parent's/guardian's signature

LESSON 4
Making Decisions

At the end of this lesson . . .

. . . you will have further developed your decision-making skills.

Key Words
- Decision
- Process
- Consequences

Keyskill
- Managing Myself

Making *decisions*

Not all decisions have serious consequences, but there are some decisions in life that are difficult to make. Some of the choices we make can affect our lives long after we have made them. Here are six decision-making styles that young people often adopt.

- **Look at the advantages and disadvantages**: Carefully consider your options and the consequences of your actions, and then make your decision.
- **Go along with everyone else**: Do what everyone else is doing; follow the crowd.
- **Go with your gut feeling**: Make your decision based on how you feel.
- **Ask for help**: Take advice from somebody you trust.
- **Act on impulse**: Make a snap decision; act without thinking.
- **Bide your time**: Put off making the decision for as long as possible.

Pair Activity

In pairs, discuss and write down which decision-making style is most appropriate for each of the following decisions. Give reasons for your answers.

Will I wear the blue or the red top?

Go with your gut

Will I spend my last five euros on a takeaway or will I get a taxi home?

look at the advantages and disadvantages

Will I take Higher Level or Ordinary Level maths for my Junior Certificate?

ask for help

Will I drink alcohol with my friends or not?

Go with your gut feeling

Will I try to include the new student or will I choose to ignore them?

Will I join the basketball team or the soccer team?

_____

_____

Will I copy my homework from a friend or will I own up to not having done it?

_____

_____

I think my parents will still be out when I get home, so will I stay out with my friends an extra hour?

_____

_____

_____

Will I go to the cinema with Sarah, as promised, or will I go to the school party?

_____

_____

_____

ABCDE decision-making model

Sometimes we have to make a difficult decision and it is good to have a strategy to help with this. The following model can help you with making good decisions.

A → **Assess** the problem
What decision has to be made?

B → **Brainstorm** the solutions
List the different options you can choose

C → **Consider** the consequences of each decision
What are the consequences of each of the choices you could make?

D → **Decide** and act
Decide what you want to do

E → **Evaluate** your decision
Explain the pros and cons of your choice and reflect on your decision

Individual Activity

Let's apply the ABCDE model to your life.

Think of a decision in your own life. Use the steps from the ABCDE model to help you.

Assess the decision: what decision has to be made?

_____

_____

_____

Brainstorm the solutions: what are the different options you could choose?

_____

_____

_____

Consider the consequences of each decision: what are the consequences for your future of each possible choice?

_____

_____

_____

Decide and act: decide what you want to do.

_____

_____

_____

Evaluate the consequences: explain the pros and cons of your choice and reflect on your decision.

_____

_____

_____

Learning *Keepsake*

Three things I have learned about decision-making are:

1. _____
2. _____
3. _____

As a result of what I have learned about decision-making, I will:

_____
_____
_____

_____ has shared this Learning Keepsake with me _____

Name of student   Parent's/guardian's signature

Topic Review

Date / /

In this topic I learned about

_____

This topic is useful to me in my life because

_____
_____

In this topic I liked

_____
_____

In this topic I did not like

_____
_____

I would like to find out more about

_____
_____

Key Skills I have used in this topic are:

- ☐ Managing myself
- ☐ Staying well
- ☐ Communicating
- ☐ Being creative
- ☐ Working with others
- ☐ Managing information and thinking

* Are you up for the challenge?

Design a resource for young people to help them make decisions.

TOPIC 2

My Rights and the Rights of Others

- Lesson 5 Group Work
- Lesson 6 Family Ties

LESSON 5
Group Work

At the end of this lesson . . .

. . . you will know more about working successfully as a member of a group.

Key Words
- Ground rules
- Class contract

Keyskill
- Working with others

Class Activity

This is Ms Doyle's SPHE class. She has written some words on the board that can help the class run well. Discuss as a class how each word would help an SPHE class work efficiently.

Confidentiality

Respect

Responsibility

Freedom

Participation

Organisation

Punctuality

Group Activity

Think about the meanings of the words. Select five that are most important to the group and write down five ground rules that your group thinks are important for SPHE class. Write the rules below.

1. Respect - there needs to be respect so everyone feels accepted
2. Confidentiality - everyones business is kept inside the classroom
3. Organisation - have your things for class
4. Responsibility - take responsibility when you are wrong
5. Freedom

Class Activity

One person from each group must report the group's ideas back to the class. Try to come to an agreement over the ground rules the class would like to implement. Remember to include the teacher too.

Once the whole class has agreed on the ground rules, write them in the contract below. You must then get everyone in the class – and the teacher – to sign the contract to show that they agree with it.

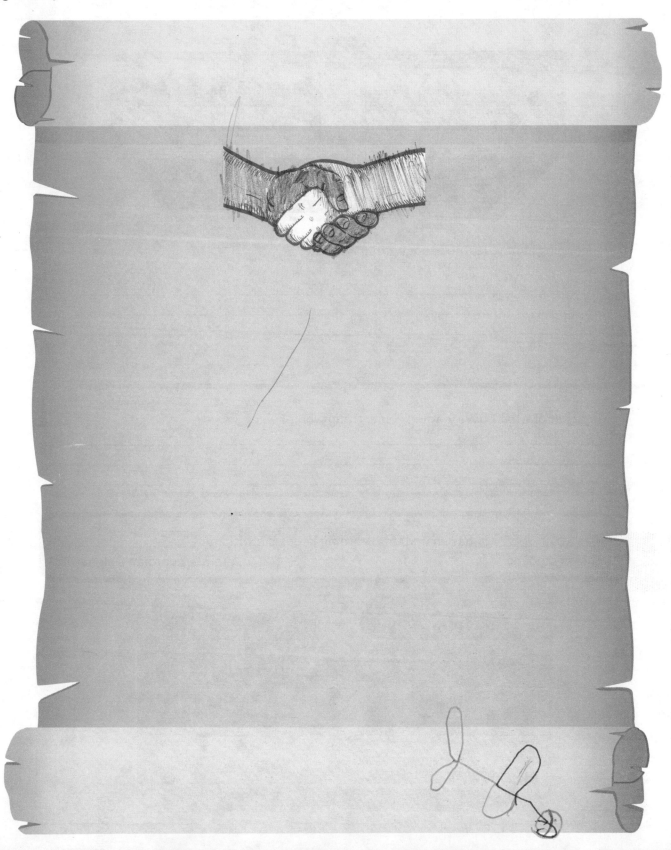

Learning *Keepsake*

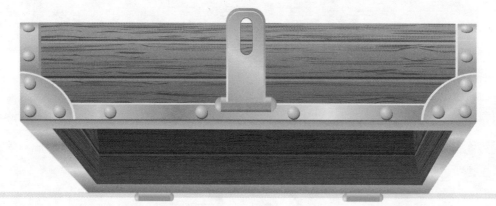

Three things I have learned about group work are:

1. _____
2. _____
3. _____

As a result of what I have learned about group work, I will:

_____

_____

_____

____Conor_____ has shared this Learning Keepsake with me _____

Name of student   Parent's/guardian's signature

LESSON 6
Family Ties

At the end of this lesson . . .
. . . you will have examined the different relationships in your family.

Key Word
- Relationships

Keyskill
- Working with Others

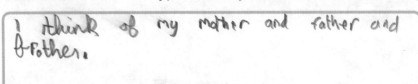

- Brainstorm what the word 'family' means to your group.
- Describe the different types of family that there are in our society.

> I think of my mother and father and brother.

Read the following dialogue about the Murphy family.

It is Tuesday morning in the Murphy household and the family are getting ready for school and for work.

Mrs Murphy	Eoin, it's ten to eight – are you out of bed yet?
Eoin	I'm waiting for Brid to come out of the bathroom so I can have a shower.
Mrs Murphy	Well, come down and eat your breakfast while you're waiting; we don't have that much time left.
Brid	(*shouting to her mother from the bathroom*) Is my hockey gear ready? I've a match today.
Mrs Murphy	I don't know; I told you to get organised last night.
Mr Murphy	(passing Brid on the stairs) What are you doing with all that make-up and those earrings going to school? I thought we'd talked about that already.
Brid	Oh, Dad, relax. Everyone in school wears them. I don't have time to take them off now anyway, we're in a hurry.
Mrs Murphy	Eoin, where are you going? Sit down and finish your cereal.
Eoin	I'd better hurry up and have my shower because we have to leave in fifteen minutes. Will you make me a sandwich for my lunch?
Mr Murphy	I thought you'd agreed to make your own lunches every night, Eoin. Your mother has enough to do.
Eoin	But, Dad, I had training until six last night and then I had after-school study until ten – I was wrecked when I got home. Can I have a fiver for a roll instead?
Mrs Murphy	I'll make you a sandwich this time, Eoin, but you'll have to be more organised tomorrow. I'm not wasting my hard-earned money on rolls and sweets.
Eoin	Can I have two euros to get something before study so? I'm always starving after school.
Mr Murphy	No! Bring an extra sandwich. Now hurry up because I have to leave on time this morning – I don't want to get stuck in the traffic.
Brid	I need two euros for the bus to the hockey match.
Mr Murphy	Here you are. Now, good luck in the match. I'll text you later to see how you got on.
Eoin	Hey! That's not fair! How come she gets two euros and I don't?

1. Make a list of the different sources of conflict in the Murphy household.

- The children not being organised
- The lunches not being ready
- Brid getting €2 and Tom getting nothing

2. Make a list of other issues that can cause conflict in families.

- One sibling is liked better then another.
- Not getting up in time for school.
- Being unorganised

3. Pick one of the issues that can cause conflict in family life and discuss how it could be resolved.

ISSUE	HOW TO RESOLVE
being unorganised	Prepare the day before

Family life

There are many benefits to being part of a family, including housing, food, clothing, health care, education, companionship and love.

As well as having privileges, you also have certain responsibilities to your family.

These responsibilities include: looking out for all other family members; taking care of siblings; visiting older relations; and doing household chores.

Sometimes conflicts can arise within families because of expectations around privileges and responsibilities. Here are some guidelines to help you get on better with your family.

1. Be helpful: tidy your room, help with the laundry and look after younger siblings if needed.
2. Be thoughtful: if you need to borrow something, ask first and then return it in good condition.
3. Show your parents/carers you can behave responsibly: always let them know where you are and what time to expect you home.
4. Don't tell lies: keep your parents'/carers' trust.
5. Take time to chat to all family members. Spend some time with them – even if it is just eating a meal together or watching a DVD.

My responsibilities at home

1. Write down some of the tasks and responsibilities you have in your family.

Day the dishes

Empty the dishwasher

Hoover

2. In the box below, write down how your role has changed in your family as you have grown older.

~~father + 2~~
As I've got older I've been trusted with more ~~jobs~~ such as hoovering

Learning *Keepsake*

Three things I have learned about family life are:

1. How to earn more trust
2. How to avoid conflicts in my family
3. How to help out

As a result of what I have learned about family life, I will:

_____

_____

_____ has shared this Learning Keepsake with me _____

Name of student   Parent's/guardian's signature

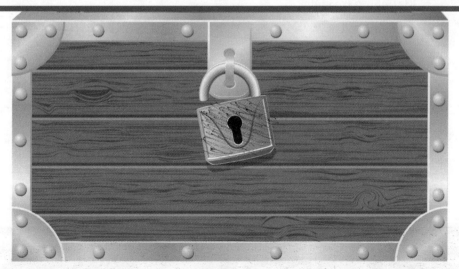

Topic Review

Date / /

In this topic I learned about

Family life

This topic is useful to me in my life because

I can use it to ~~help~~ avoid conflicts on my family

In this topic I liked

In this topic I did not like

I would like to find out more about

Key Skills I have used in this topic are:

- ☑ Managing myself
- ☐ Staying well
- ☑ Communicating
- ☐ Being creative
- ☐ Working with others
- ☑ Managing information and thinking

*Are you up for the challenge?

Choose a family member you really admire and create their biography. Include photographs and interesting details about this person. Present your biography to the class in an interesting way.

Respectful Communication

- Lesson 7 Assertive Communication

LESSON 7
Assertive Communication

At the end of this lesson . . .
. . . you will have practised assertive communication skills
. . . you will be aware of the appropriate uses of assertive communication.

Key Words
- Communication
- Passive
- Aggressive
- Assertive

 # Keyskill
- Communication

Standing up for yourself

In first year you learned about the difference between assertive, aggressive and passive behaviour. Look at the table to remind yourself what each of these means.

Passive	Assertive	Aggressive

You do: • rely on others to guess what you want • hope that you will get what you want • hide your feelings • sigh, sulk, hint, wish • feel trampled on	**You do:** • ask for what you want • behave openly and directly • believe in yourself • ask confidently and without undue anxiety • look for 'win–win' situations	**You do:** • try to get what you want in any way that works • often cause bad feelings in others • threaten, cajole, use sarcasm, bully, manipulate, fight
You don't: • ask for what you want express your feelings • usually get what you want • feel good about yourself	**You don't:** • violate other people's rights • expect other people to guess what you want • freeze with anxiety	**You don't:** • respect the fact that others have rights too • look for 'win–win' situations

Although assertive communication skills are very important, there are times when it is not appropriate to use them. If a person is unwell, has received some bad news or is going through a rough patch, you may need to be sensitive to what they are feeling. At other times an assertive response could be putting your safety at risk, so you need to assess the situation.

Individual Activity

Scenario 1

You buy a new coat. After returning home you notice that it's ripped under the arm. When you return to the store the shop assistant claims that you damaged it. What would be an aggressive response in this situation?

Give out to them

Scenario 2

You are hanging out with your friends outside your house. A neighbour comes out of her house and asks you to move on because you're keeping her child awake. What would be an aggressive response in this situation?

To fight the woman or bully

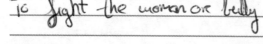

Scenario 3

Your teacher finds your name written on the desk. He accuses you of doing it. What is a passive response in this situation?

Accept the blame

Scenario 4

You are going to a disco. You are wearing a new jacket. When you meet your friend she tells you she does not think it suits you. What would be a passive response?

To take the jacket off and get a new one

Scenario 5

You are in your local shop and you see someone shoplifting. The person looks quite tough and notices that you are looking at them. What would be an assertive response in this situation?

Let her off

Scenario 6

You are organising your birthday party. You've heard at school that one of the boys in your class assumes he is invited. You hadn't intended inviting him. What would be an assertive response?

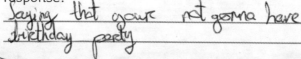

Saying that your not gonna have a birthday party

Role Play

In small groups select one of the scenarios above and role play an assertive response.

_____

_____

Tips for assertive communication

1. Stand or sit up straight.

2. Make eye contact but don't glare at the other person.

3. Keep your voice calm – do not whine and do not shout.

4. Wear a firm but not aggressive expression.

5. Use clear, direct statements, e.g. 'Would you please return my top?' rather than 'Would you mind returning my top?'

6. Say what you have to say and stick to it.

7. When refusing a request, say no clearly. If you are unsure, do not make a rushed decision – say you will think about it and get back to the other person.

Learning to be assertive can benefit you in many areas of your life. It can help you to:

1. Express positive feelings well.
2. Express negative feelings well.
3. Stand up for your rights.

In each of the areas below, reflect on how assertive you are. For each area in which you are assertive, tick the appropriate box.

	Excellent	Very good	Good	Average	Poor
1. Expressing your feelings					
Telling someone you appreciate them	☐	☑	☑	☐	☐
Giving compliments	☐	☐	☑	☐	☐
Receiving compliments	☐	☐	☐	☑	☐
Starting conversations	☐	☑	☐	☐	☐
2. Expressing negative feelings					
Showing that you are annoyed	☐	☐	☐	☐	☑
Showing that you are hurt	☐	☐	☐	☐	☑
Showing that you are sorry	☐	☐	☑	☐	☐
3. Standing up for your rights					
Making complaints	☐	☐	☐	☐	☑
Refusing requests; saying no	☐	☐	☐	☐	☑
Giving your opinion	☐	☐	☐	☑	☐
Refusing to be put down	☐	☐	☐	☐	☑

Write about a time when you acted:

1. Assertively _____

2. Passively I seen a man shoplifting and I let him off

3. Aggressively _____

How did you feel afterwards?

1. _____

2. _____

3. _____

Could you have said or done anything differently? How would this have helped?

1. _____

2. _____

3. _____

Learning *Keepsake*

Three things I have learned about assertive communication are:

1. _____
2. _____
3. _____

As a result of what I have learned about assertive communication, I will:

_____
_____
_____

_____ has shared this Learning Keepsake with me _____
Name of student   Parent's/guardian's signature

Topic Review

Date / /

In this topic I learned about

_____

This topic is useful to me in my life because

_____
_____

In this topic I liked

_____
_____

In this topic I did not like

_____
_____

I would like to find out more about

_____
_____

Key Skills I have used in this module are:

- ☐ Managing myself
- ☐ Staying well
- ☐ Communicating
- ☐ Being creative
- ☐ Working with others
- ☐ Managing information and thinking

*Are you up for the challenge?

In pairs, devise a 10-part quiz for young people to determine whether or not they are assertive communicators. Give the quiz to your class and show the results on a pie chart.

Having a Friend and Being a Friend

- Lesson 8 The Changing Nature of Friendship

LESSON 8

The Changing Nature of Friendship

At the end of this lesson . . .

. . . you will have reflected on the changing nature of friendship.

Key Words
- Acquaintances
- Confidential

 # Keyskill
- Working with Others

Types of *friendship*

Read the following definitions and write a list of your close friends, your friends and your acquaintances.

Acquaintances

These are the people you know to say hello to, but you would not meet up with them regularly. You do not know these people very well and they do not know you.

Social network friends

These are people you are friends with on social network sites such as Facebook.

Friendly friends

People you are friendly with and with whom you sometimes socialise. You get on well with these people, but you are not very close to them and you do not confide in them.

Close friends

Close friends are people you are close to and people you like talking to. You meet with them regularly and you can share your problems and secrets in confidence.

Individual Activity

1. What is the difference between the people who are 'friends' and the people who are 'close friends' in your list?

   friends are people that you talk to a socialise with sometimes whereas close friends are people you've known a long time and can trust

2. If you had made the list in primary school, would it be the same as it is now?

   Mostly because I've stayed close friends with some people in my primary

3. Give three reasons why changes occur in friendships.
   a) *People*
   b)
   c)

4. How do you keep in touch with friends outside school (e.g. Facebook, texting, meeting up)?

_____

_____

_____

5. How many friends do you have on your social network site(s)?

_____

6. Approximately how many of your social network friends are:

Acquaintances

Close friends

Friends

7. List the advantages and the disadvantages of having friends on social networking sites.

ADVANTAGES

DISADVANTAGES

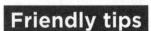

Friendly tips

- Take your time: When you meet someone new it is okay to be friendly, but wait until you know them well before confiding any secrets.
- Choose your social networking friends carefully: Remember the golden rule: treat others as you would like to be treated, even in the virtual world.
- Be trustworthy: If your friend confides in you, do not betray their confidence.
- Remember: It is natural for friendships to end – for a variety of reasons. A friendship might end because two people simply drift apart, or it might end because of a falling out. If you do fall out with a friend, it is important to remain polite and respectful. Do not try to turn other people against your old friend.

Individual Activity

Niamh and Valerie

Niamh has been friends with Valerie since primary school. It is the school colours day. Niamh spent a lot of time selecting her outfit for the day and she feels good. When she arrives at school she sees Valerie with some first years from another class. Niamh waves at the group and then goes to join them. Niamh notices the other girls start sniggering and laughing and she feels it is directed at her. What is worse, Valerie is joining in.

1. How do you think Niamh feels in this situation?

She probably feels upset embarrassed and betrayed

2. How do you think Niamh should deal with the situation?

Walk away

3. Why do you think Valerie is behaving like this to her friend?

Brian and Andy

Brian is chatting with a few friends during lunch at school when some of the lads start slagging his friend Andy. Although Brian knows that what they are saying is not true, he finds himself being dragged into the conversation.

1. How do you think Brian feels afterwards?

He probably feels guilty

2. What could Brian have done differently in this situation?

3. Have you ever found yourself in this situation? What could you do if the same thing happens in the future?

Learning *Keepsake*

Three things I have learned about friendship are:

1. Don't slag friends behind their back
2. Be a good friend
3. Be careful of social media

As a result of what I have learned about friendship, I will:

_____

_____ has shared this Learning Keepsake with me _____

Name of student   Parent/guardian's signature

Topic Review

Date / /

In this topic I learned about

_____

This topic is useful to me in my life because

_____
_____
_____

In this topic I liked

_____
_____
_____

In this topic I did not like

_____
_____
_____

I would like to find out more about

_____
_____

Key Skills I have used in this topic are:

- ☐ Managing myself
- ☐ Staying well
- ☐ Communicating
- ☐ Being creative
- ☐ Working with others
- ☐ Managing information and thinking

*Are you up for the challenge?

Devise a survey to find out the average number of social network friends each student in your class has.

Anti-bullying

- Lesson 9 Cyberbullying
- Lesson 10 Feeling Threatened and Staying Safe Online

LESSON 9
Cyberbullying

At the end of this lesson . . .

. . . you will have identified the characteristics of cyberbullying

. . . you will realise the damaging effects cyberbullying has on the victim

. . . you will know the best way to deal with cyberbullying.

Key Words
- Cyberbullying
- Characteristics
- Behaviour

Keyskill
- Staying Well

Class Activity

Brainstorm the different ways in which people can be cyberbullied.

Types of cyberbullying

Pair Activity

Read the following stories about cyberbullying and answer the questions.

Text Messaging

Sadee was being bullied at school. When she woke up on Saturday morning there were 20 hurtful messages on her mobile from people she didn't know.

1. How do you think Sadee felt?

Hurt

2. What do you think Sadee should do?

Tell a friend

Social Networking

A group of boys from school created a fake Facebook page about a male teacher in their school. Different students posted spiteful and nasty comments on the page. You have heard about this page.

1. How do you think the teacher would feel if he saw this page?

He would feel hurt and upset

2. What do you think you should do?

Stolen Identity

Jane's friends were at her house and they were online. When Jane went to the kitchen to make tea, she left her Facebook page open, and her friends decided to send a spiteful message to Jane's cousin Clara, who is also in their class. The next day Clara approached Jane about the matter.

1. How do you think Jane feels?

2. What do you think Jane should do?

_____

_____

Invasion of Privacy

Jakub took a picture of Christian in the showers after the match. He then sent the pictures to several of their friends and before long it was uploaded to a number of Facebook pages.

1. How do you think Christian feels?

_____

2. What do you think Christian should do?

_____

_____

Social Exclusion

Emma has a large circle of friends. Belinda appears to be the leader of the group, but she doesn't seem to really like Emma. Emma has asked to be Facebook friends with a number of girls from the group and they have ignored her request. She thinks this is because Belinda doesn't like her.

1. How do you think Emma feels?

_____

2. What do you think Emma should do?

_____

_____

Threatening Behaviour

When Allanah broke up with Ivan he sent her many threatening and hurtful messages. He spread nasty stories about her and he posted an inappropriate photo of her online, as well as her email address and mobile number.

1. How do you think Allanah feels?

_____

2. What do you think Allanah should do?

_____

_____

www.watchyourspace.ie

Advice for dealing with cyberbullying

Remember: it is not your fault

Do not send a nasty message back

Save the messages and record the dates

Tell someone you trust

Report it to the website or phone company

Block the person as a friend or a contact

Remember: there is help

Report it to the Gardaí

Weblink

Watch the video on Cyberbullying by Childnet International on www.youtube.com

Learning *Keepsake*

Three things I have learned about cyberbullying are:

1. _____
2. _____
3. _____

As a result of what I have learned about cyberbullying, I will:

_____
_____
_____

_____ has shared this Learning Keepsake with me _____

Name of student   Parent's/guardian's signature

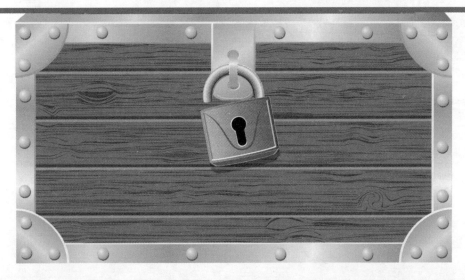

LESSON 10
Feeling Threatened and Staying Safe Online

At the end of this lesson . . .

. . . you will be more aware of your responsibilities for your own safety and the safety of others online.

Key Words

- Privacy
- Responsibility
- Actions
- Consequences

Keyskill

- Staying Well

What's your **password?**

No one would ever guess mine – it's my dog's name and the year I was born

No one would ever guess mine – it's my favourite boy band

You probably remember as a child being warned about talking to strangers. By now you have probably developed the basic skills around personal safety – you wouldn't go out after school and hand out your private information on leaflets to people passing by the school.

However, lots of people think it's okay to post private information online, where even strangers might have access to it. Modern technology can distance us from reality and it is important to realise that online actions have consequences.

 Individual Activity

Complete this questionnaire about staying safe online.

	Yes	No
Have you ever put private information about another person on a social networking site without their permission?		
Have you ever given away your personal details online (e.g. phone number, email address, street address, etc.)?		
Have you ever posted or shared secrets or embarrassing information about yourself or another person online?		
Have you ever been told something in confidence and then passed it on online?		
Have you ever posted pictures of someone without their permission online?		
Have you ever tricked someone into revealing a secret and then posted it online?		
Are there photos of you online?		
Do you share information online with people you don't really know?		
Have you ever added people to your friends list whom you have never met face to face?		
Have you ever sent personal information to someone you have never met face to face?		
Have you ever arranged to meet someone you met online?		

Class Activity

Discuss your answers with the class.

Group Activity

Brainstorm how you think what we write or post online can affect our personal safety.

How to stay safe online

Advice for using social networking sites

Treat people you meet online with the same respect that you would like to be given and the same respect you give others when you meet them in person.

Don't give out private information such as passwords, PIN numbers, addresses, phone numbers or personal details. Private information should be kept private – it can be used for harm on the internet.

Think before you post personal pictures online. Remember, pictures will be online for ever, so be sure that you would be comfortable with your parents, grandparents, teachers, employers seeing them this year, next year or in 30 years' time.

Save or print a copy of any messages or conversations that are a threat to your safety.

Don't post pictures of other people without their permission. Don't give out other people's email address, mobile number or other information to people you meet on the internet.

Learn how to block and report any messages that are distasteful, hurtful or not appropriate.

Realise that online conversations are not private. Other people can copy, print and share any pictures or comments you post.

If you use instant messaging, don't accept messages from people you don't know, don't add people to your friends list unless you know them personally, and if you do, limit the information you share with them.

Don't say or post anything that would cause you embarrassment in the future. As a general rule, if you wouldn't say it to your gran or grandad, don't say it online.

 **Weblink** – www.thinkb4uclick.ie
www.webwise.ie

Individual Activity

There are many slogans out there that help raise awareness about staying safe online, for example 'ThinkB4UClick', 'Think before you upload', 'Watch Your Space'.

Now create your own personal slogan to raise awareness about staying safe online.

Learning *Keepsake*

Three things I have learned about staying safe online are:

1. _____
2. _____
3. _____

As a result of what I have learned about staying safe online, I will:

_____
_____
_____

_____ has shared this Learning Keepsake with me _____
Name of student   Parent's/guardian's signature

Topic Review

Date / /

In this topic I learned about

_____

This topic is useful to me in my life because

_____

_____

In this topic I liked

_____

_____

In this topic I did not like

_____

_____

I would like to find out more about

_____

_____

Key Skills I have used in this topic are:

☐ Managing myself

☐ Staying well

☐ Communicating

☐ Being creative

☐ Working with others

☐ Managing information and thinking

*Are you up for the challenge?

Complete a project titled 'Staying safe online'.

TOPIC 6

Being Healthy

- Lesson 11 Body Care and Body Image
- Lesson 12 Feeling Unwell
- Lesson 13 Water Safety
- Lesson 14 Accidents at Home and at School

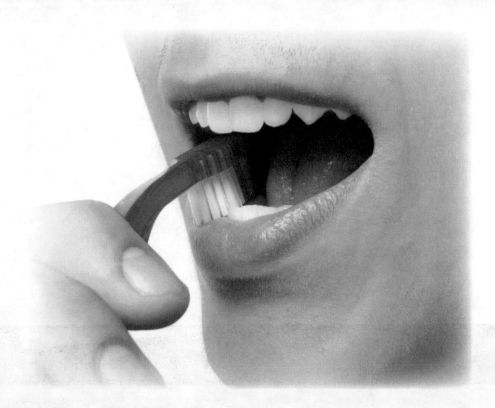

LESSON 11

Body Care and Body Image

At the end of this lesson . . .

. . . you will have reviewed the importance of personal hygiene and how to achieve it

. . . you will understand the link between body image and personal hygiene.

Key Words
- Personal
- Hygiene
- Unkempt

Keyskill
- Staying Well

The terrible *twins*

Read the stories below about Becky and Brandon and answer the questions that follow.

Becky

Becky leaves it until the last minute to get up every morning. Sometimes she doesn't have time to wash or brush her teeth before going to school. On cold mornings she leaves her pyjamas on under her uniform. Becky showers and washes her hair once a week. When her hair gets greasy she uses dry shampoo. She wears make-up, but sometimes she is too tired to take it off at night. She doesn't always put her clothes out on time to be washed. She sometimes has to pick up clothes from her bedroom floor to wear – including underwear and socks.

Brandon

Brandon spends a lot of time in front of the mirror squeezing spots, but he doesn't clean his fingernails. His mother tries to encourage him to wash every day, but sometimes he feels too tired. This means that he has smelly feet and armpits. Brandon plays a lot of sport, but he doesn't wash his sports gear until the end of every school term. He doesn't always shower after training or matches, and he has often gone to bed with muck still on him. He lost his toothbrush two weeks ago when he went to stay with a friend and now he cleans his teeth with his finger.

Individual Activity

Do you think Brenda and Brandon's hygiene practices are normal? Give reasons for your answer.

_____

_____

_____

How do you think people might react to Brenda and Brandon?

_____

_____

_____

Do you think their hygiene practices could have an affect how they feel about themselves?

_____

What might cause someone to have poor hygiene standards?

_____

Is it difficult to give someone advice about their personal hygiene? Give reasons for your answer.

_____

_____

_____

Class Activity

Share your answers with your teacher and the class.

Group Activity

In groups, review what rules you learned about personal hygiene in first year.

Skin care		
Foot care		
Dental care		
Hair care		

Nail care

Individual Activity

You are going on an outdoor adventure week with a group from school. There will be a lot of physical activity during the day. You need to pack everything that you will need for your own personal hygiene.

In the back pack below, draw or write in all the things you will bring with you.

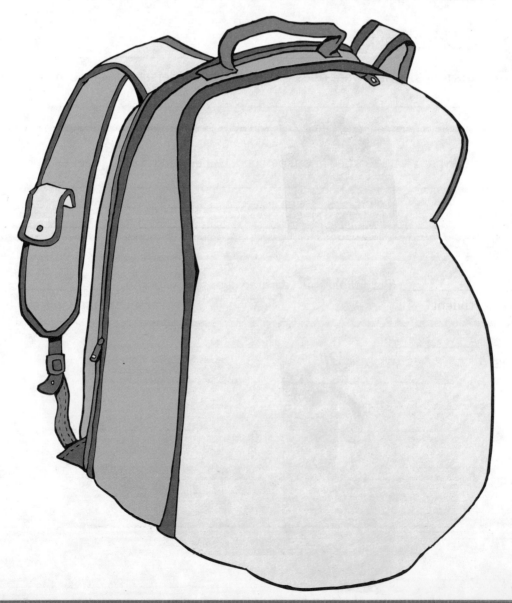

Learning *Keepsake*

Three things I have learned about personal hygiene and body image are:

1. _____
2. _____
3. _____

As a result of what I have learned about personal hygiene and body image, I will:

_____
_____
_____

_____ has shared this Learning Keepsake with me _____
Name of student   Parent's/guardian's signature

LESSON 12

Feeling Unwell

At the end of this lesson . . .
. . . you will be able to recognise the symptoms of common illnesses
. . . you will be able to identify the causes of these illnesses
. . . and you will appreciate the importance of getting medical help and advice.

Key Words
- Disease
- Illness
- Symptoms

Keyskill
- Staying Well

Look at the picture below and circle possible causes of illness or infection.

Group Activity

1. Write down a list of hygiene guidelines under the following headings.
2. State what infections or illnesses can be prevented by following your guidelines.

a) Washing your hands.

1. _____
   _____
   _____

2. _____
   _____
   _____

b) Flies on food.

1. _____
   _____
   _____

2. _____
   _____
   _____

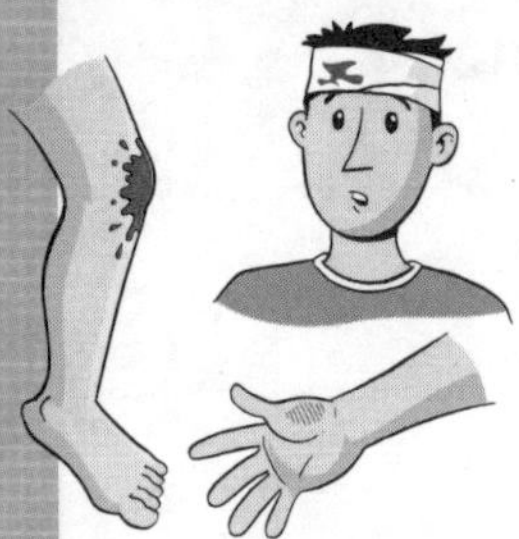

c) Cuts and open wounds.

1. _____
   _____
   _____

2. _____
   _____
   _____

d) Pets.

1. _____
   _____
   _____

2. _____
   _____
   _____

e) Eating fruit and vegetables.

1. _____
   _____
   _____

2. _____
   _____
   _____

f) Coughing and sneezing.

1. _____
   _____
   _____

2. _____
   _____
   _____

Some common illnesses

Not all illnesses are caused by poor hygiene. As a teenager you may suffer from or know someone who has experienced some of the following illnesses or conditions.

Acne

This is a skin condition that causes spots or pimples on the upper torso, neck and face. It can be mild, moderate or severe. Sometimes it is caused by a bacterial infection, but it can also be caused by excess sebum production or hormonal changes. Mild acne can be treated with over-the-counter products from a pharmacy; more severe acne can be treated by a GP.

Iron deficiency anaemia

Anaemia occurs when a person doesn't have the normal amount of red blood cells or if the person doesn't have enough haemoglobin. Red blood cells are produced in the body's bone marrow and carry oxygen around the body. They contain haemoglobin, a protein that holds on to oxygen.

In order to make enough haemoglobin, the body needs to have plenty of iron. A healthy and balanced diet ensures that the body has adequate amounts of iron. Girls need extra iron in their diet because they are more prone to anaemia; this is due to menstruation. Signs of anaemia include tiredness, lethargy (lack of energy) and shortness of breath. If you suspect you have anaemia it is important to go to your GP.

Meningitis

The meninges are the protective membranes that cover the brain and spinal cord. Meningitis is a disease which causes inflammation of the meninges. It can be caused by a bacterial or viral infection. Some of the symptoms of meningitis are:

- a very bad headache that won't go away
- neck/back stiffness
- sensitivity to light
- nausea or vomiting
- body aches
- fever
- drowsiness
- feeling confused.

If you suspect you or someone else has meningitis it is important to contact a doctor immediately.

Cold sores

Cold sores are caused by the Herpes simplex virus 1 (HSV-1).They are small and painful blisters that usually show up on or around a person's lips. Your pharmacist will be able to supply suitable creams to treat cold sores.

Warts and verrucas

Warts are hard lumps of skin that are caused by a virus. They usually appear on the hands and feet. Verrucas are warts that usually develop on the soles of the feet. Anyone can get warts and although they are unsightly they can be easily treated. It is important to treat them quickly as they are infectious.

Other common illnesses that teenagers may experience include allergies, asthma and migraine. It is important to seek medical help for all these conditions.

Project

Below is a list of minor ailments. Choose one from the list, and research its symptoms and treatment. Try to find out about alternative remedies as well as the more conventional ones.

- Colds
- Headlice
- Dandruff
- Sunburn
- Flu
- Diarrhoea
- Cough

- Sore throat
- Headache
- Menstrual cramps
- Hay fever
- Indigestion
- Athlete's foot

Learning *Keepsake*

Three things I have learned about feeling unwell are:

1. To get it checked if you suspect it serious
2. The symptoms of certain illnesses
3. How the illness starts

As a result of what I have learned about feeling unwell, I will:

Be more aware of illness

_____ has shared this Learning Keepsake with me _____

Name of student   Parent's/guardian's signature

LESSON 13

Water Safety

At the end of this lesson . . .
. . . you will know how to keep safe while swimming.

Key Words
- Difficulty
- Parallel
- Safety equipment

 # Keyskill
- Staying Well

Water Safety

Did you know that, on average, 140 people drown in Ireland each year? Most of these tragic deaths happen inland, in rivers and lakes, on farms and in and around homes, and these accidents are preventable.

Each of the cartoons below has a safety message about swimming. Match each cartoon with the relevant safety message. The first one has been done for you.

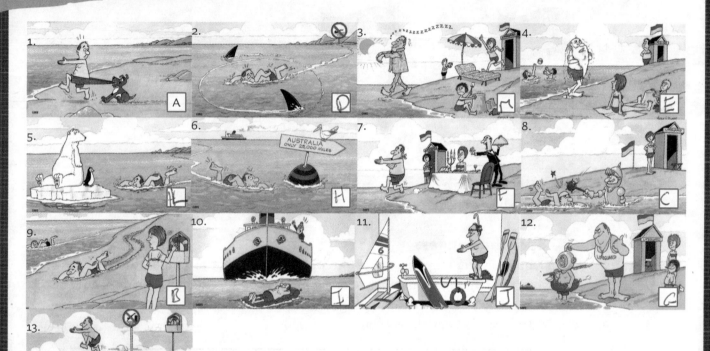

A. Don't swim alone.

B. Swim parallel and close to the shore

C. Don't be a bully

D. Don't swim in strange places

E. Don't stay in the water too long

F. Don't swim just after eating

G. Obey the lifeguard

H. Don't swim out to sea

I. Never use air mattresses

J. Learn to use equipment before trying it out

K. Pay attention to signs on the beach

L. Don't swim out after anything drifting

M. Don't swim if you are feeling tired

Weblink
www.aquaattack.ie

As a class, discuss what reason is behind each safety message.

The water safety code

Every stretch of open water (beaches, ponds, rivers and lakes) has its own set of dangers. Before going swimming it is important to follow the water safety code:

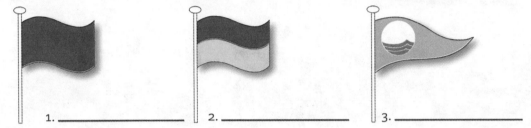

1. _____ 2. _____ 3. _____

1.   Spot the dangers.
2.   Take advice.
3.   Don't go it alone.
4.   Learn how to help.

1.   Spot the dangers

Before going swimming you should look out for any potential dangers and look for any sources of information or help. For example, is there a lifeguard on duty and, if so, where are they? Are there warning signs?
Write down any other dangers you need to spot.

_____
_____
_____

2.   Take advice

If the lifeguard is on duty, ask him or her about possible dangers. Do not go swimming in a place you do not know.
Look at the flags below. What do they mean?

3.   Don't go it alone

Never swim on your own and always tell someone where you are going.

4.   Learn how to help

Identify what the below flags mean.

- Call the lifeguard for help or get someone to call 999.
- Throw a safety aid from the land to the person.
- If they are close, reach out with a branch or an oar.
- Don't get into the water.

Weblink

www.iws.ie

 Individual Activity

Design a billboard advertisement that raises awareness about water safety.

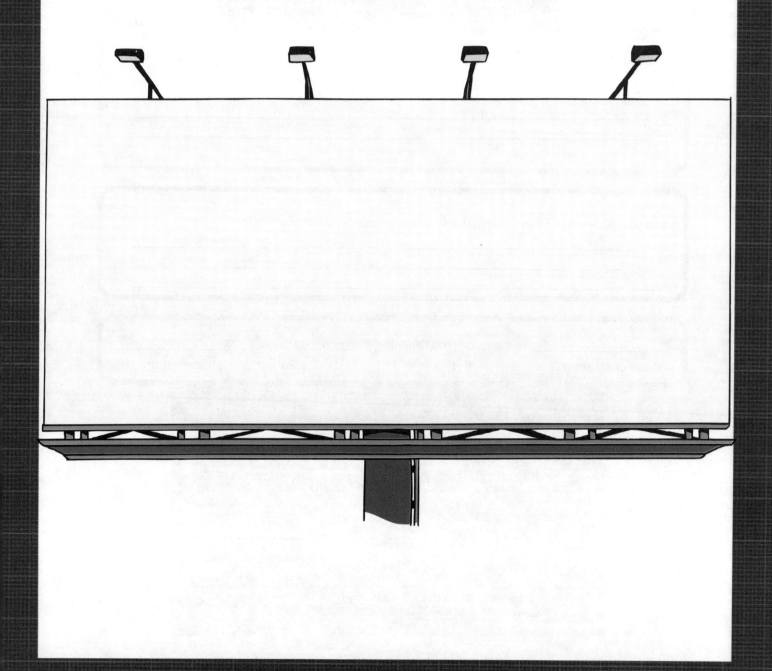

Learning *Keepsake*

Three things I have learned about water safety are:

1. _____
2. _____
3. _____

As a result of what I have learned about water safety, I will:

_____

_____

_____

_____ has shared this Learning Keepsake with me _____

Name of student   Parent's/guardian's signature

LESSON 14

Accidents at Home and at School

At the end of this lesson . . .
. . . you will have a greater awareness of safety at home and at school.

Key Words
- Accident
- Prevention
- Emergency

 # Keyskill
- Staying Safe

Pair Activity

Look at the pictures below. For each picture, list what accidents or injuries could occur and suggest how they can be avoided.

Possible dangers:

_____

_____

Could be avoided by: _____

_____

Possible dangers:

_____

_____

Could be avoided by: _____

_____

Possible dangers:

_____

_____

Could be avoided by: _____

_____

Possible dangers:

_____

_____

Could be avoided by: _____

_____

Possible dangers:

_____

_____

Could be avoided by: _____

_____

Possible dangers:

_____

_____

Could be avoided by: _____

_____

Possible dangers:

_____

Could be avoided by: _____

_____

Possible dangers:

_____

Could be avoided by: _____

_____

 Group Activity

Write down five tips to make your home and school a safer place.

Home

1. _____
2. _____
3. _____
4. _____
5. _____

School

1. _____
2. _____
3. _____
4. _____
5. _____

Personal safety

To prevent accidents happening, possible risks and safety hazards must be identified and removed. It is important to take responsibility for your environment and your behaviour in order to reduce the risk of accident and injury to yourself and others. It is also important to know how to treat minor injuries that may occur.

Burns

There are three types of burn:

1. First-degree burns: only the top layer of the skin is damaged. These burns are caused by brief contact with heat.
2. Second-degree burns: the damage is deeper and usually causes blisters and redness.

3. Third-degree burns: very deep burns. While they may be painless initially, they may need to be treated with skin grafts.

Treatment

Anyone who suffers a second- or third-degree burn should go to hospital straight away. If someone has a first-degree burn (or a second-degree burn and you cannot get them to hospital immediately) follow these steps:

- Remove any clothing from around the area; but do not remove any clothing that is stuck to the skin.
- Run cool water over the burn for about ten minutes.
- Remove rings or watches, which may be difficult to remove if the area becomes swollen later.
- Apply a gauze bandage.

Do not:
- break blisters
- apply lotions, creams or ointments to large burned areas.

Poisons

Treatment

If you suspect someone has taken a poison and they are still conscious, you should:
- Stay calm and act quickly.
- Seek medical advice as soon as possible.
- Find out as much as possible about the poison they have taken.
- Bring a sample of the poison or the vomit to the hospital.
- If a chemical has splashed into the eyes, wash the eyes with tap water for 15 minutes.
- Wash any skin that was in contact with the poison with soap and water.
- Call the Poisons Information Centre on (01) 809 2166 (8 a.m.–10 p.m.).
- Always take the product container with you to the telephone or to the GP or hospital.

Do not:
- make the person vomit.

Nosebleeds

Treatment
- Put on gloves.
- Lean the person's head forward.
- Pinch or get the person themselves to pinch the soft part of their nose.
- Apply pressure for about 10 minutes.
- Advise the patient to breath through their mouth.
- Seek medical advice if bleeding occurs for longer than 30 minutes or if bleeding recurs.

Do not:
- tilt your head back
- blow your nose – and don't blow your nose for some hours.

Sprains and strains

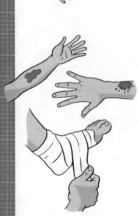

If you are unsure whether the injury is a sprain or a fracture, you should treat it as a fracture.

Treatment for sprains and strains is RICE:
- **R** – Rest the injured muscle.
- **I** – Ice. Apply a cold compress for 20 minutes and keep reapplying: this helps to reduce swelling.
- **C** – Compression. Apply a firm bandage to reduce swelling.
- **E** – Elevate. Raise the injured area to reduce blood flow.

Fainting

Fainting occurs when there is a lack of blood reaching the brain.

Treatment

If someone is feeling faint:

- Get them to sit down and place their head between their knees.
- Tell them to take deep breaths.
- Allow them to sit up slowly.
- Offer sips of water.
- Alternatively, get the person to lie down with their legs raised.

Cuts and wounds

Most cuts can be easily treated at home, but you should seek medical advice for deeper cuts and wounds that do not stop bleeding.

For minor cuts:
- Put on gloves.
- If the cut is dirty, clean it with a sterile wipe or run water over it.
- If there is a lot of bleeding, apply pressure to the wound until the bleeding stops.
- Raise the wounded area where necessary.
- Dress the affected area with a sterile pad and bandage.

First aid

First aid is the first treatment given to a person who has been injured or taken ill. A basic knowledge of first aid can be very helpful. There are many courses available throughout Ireland – why not find out about one in your area?

Weblink

www.redcross.ie

Pair Activity

In pairs, practise some of the treatments for the minor injuries listed above.

Learning *Keepsake*

Three things I have learned about safety at home and at school are:

1. _____
2. _____
3. _____

As a result of what I have learned about safety, I will:

_____
_____
_____

_____ has shared this Learning Keepsake with me _____

Name of student   Parent's/guardian's signature

Topic Review

Date / /

In this topic I learned about

_____

This topic is useful to me in my life because

_____

_____

In this topic I liked

_____

_____

In this topic I did not like

_____

_____

I would like to find out more about

_____

_____

Key Skills I have used in this topic are:

☐ Managing myself   ☐ Being creative

☐ Staying well   ☐ Working with others

☐ Communicating   ☐ Managing information and thinking

*Are you up for the challenge?

As a class, organise the following people to come and speak to you about staying safe:

1. A representative from your local branch of the Red Cross.
2. A lifeguard.
3. A spokesperson from AA Roadwatch

or

Create a radio advertisement promoting good hygiene practices among young people.

Positive Mental Health

- Lesson 15 Self-confidence
- Lesson 16 Positive and Negative Influences
- Lesson 17 Body Image

LESSON 15

Self-confidence

At the end of this lesson . . .

. . . you will have improved your skills of raising your self-esteem and the self-esteem of others.

Key Words
- Self-esteem
- Self-confidence

Keyskill
- Staying Well

Self-esteem and *self-confidence*

Self-esteem is all about how much you value yourself and how you feel about yourself overall. People with healthy self-esteem feel good about themselves, appreciate their own worth, and are proud of themselves. People with low self-esteem may be less able to recognise their qualities and accomplishments.

Self-esteem and self-confidence are linked, but they are not the same: self-confidence is about how you feel about your capabilities. You can develop skills to improve both self-esteem and self-confidence.

As a teenager you are constantly having different thoughts and feelings about different aspects of your life. These may be thoughts about:

- how you see yourself . . .

- how you judge what you do . . .

- your views of your future . . .

The thoughts we have about ourselves can affect our self-confidence.
Our thoughts can be positive, for example 'I played well in the game today,' or they can be negative, for example 'I played really badly today.'

In the thought bubble below, write down the positive and negative thoughts young people might have about themselves.

How we see ourselves	How we judge what we do	Our view of the future

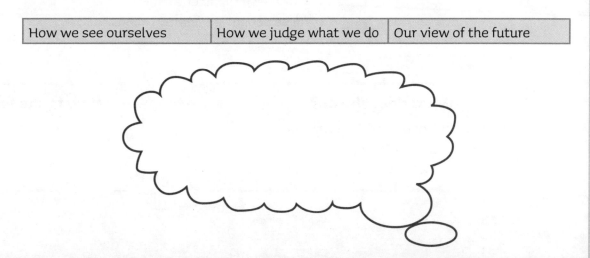

Class Activity

How we think can affect how we feel and how we behave. Read the following two reactions to a similar situation and discuss the consequences of each reaction.

Cliodhna

Cliodhna is walking down the street. She passes a group of students from her school who she is not very friendly with. One of the group passes a nasty comment about her appearance, and they all laugh.

What is she thinking?

'What they said must be true.'
'Everyone must think this about me.'
'If I wore more makeup it would help.'

What does she do?

She puts her head down.
She gets angry with her mother when she gets home.
She goes to unreasonable extremes to change.

How is she feeling?

Sad
Embarrassed
Paranoid

Orla

A few minutes later Orla, Cliodhna's friend, walks down the same street. As she passes the group they make a similar nasty remark, and they all laugh.

What is she thinking?

'They're just idiots. What they say
doesn't matter to me.'
'These people are not my friends.'

What does she do?

Surrounding herself with people who make
her feel good.
Ignoring the group's comments.

How is she feeling?

Confident
Assured
Positive

Individual Activity

As you can see, there are two – or more – reactions to every situation, and how we think can influence how we respond. Write down one negative thought a person your age might have, suggest how it might make them feel, and how they might behave.

Thought

Behaviour	Feelings

Now change the negative thought to a positive one and suggest how the positive thought affects how the person would feel and behave.

Thought

Behaviour	Feelings

Thinking positive

- Thinking negatively can make us feel bad about ourselves, reduce our self-esteem and prevent us achieving our goals.
- Thinking positively can help us to feel better about ourselves, and encourage us to achieve our goals.
- The more we listen to our negative thoughts the more we begin to believe they are true.
- We are sometimes very good at zoning in on our failures or shortcomings. In doing this we fail to recognise the good things about ourselves.
- It is also important to remember that what we say to others can affect their self-confidence. Respect for others helps you to become more confident.
- Being confident is not about being boastful or overpowering; it is about recognising your own strengths and being happy with who you are as a person.
- One way to become more confident is to talk positively to ourselves.
- Remember – Our self-esteem is affected by what we say to ourselves. We can affect the self-esteem of others by what we say to them.

Individual Activity

Design a poster for your bedroom wall to remind you of your positive qualities. The poster should include:
- something positive about yourself
- something positive you have achieved
- things or people who make you feel good about yourself
- something positive you would like to achieve
- a compliment you received in the past that has made you feel good.

Learning *Keepsake*

Three things I have learned about self-confidence are:

1. How important it is to think positively.
2. What self esteem is - how to boost your self esteem
3. How to boost others self esteem.

As a result of what I have learned about self-confidence, I will:

I will try and boost my self esteem

_____Conor_____ has shared this Learning Keepsake with me _____

Name of student   Parent's/guardian's signature

LESSON 16

Positive and Negative Influences

At the end of this lesson . . .

. . . you will have examined the positive and negative influences in your life

. . . you will be aware of the way you influence others.

Key Words

- Influence
- Positive influence
- Negative influence

Keyskill

- Working with Others

What and who influence us?

Mandy

'I get the ideas for my clothes from *Look* magazine. I changed my hairstyle last year and I based it on my favourite pop star. I started wearing make-up this year because my friends all started wearing it too. Make-up is against the school rules but I mostly get away with it. Last week I got detention, though, because I refused to wash off my mascara and eye liner. I have toned it down a little now, though, so nobody notices that I am wearing it.

'At the weekend I usually hang around the local shopping centre with my friends and we usually go to McDonald's for our lunch. I just get fries and a soft drink because I am vegetarian since I saw a documentary on TV about animal cruelty. We are all going to the cinema next week to see the new horror film that everyone likes on Facebook.

'My favourite music is indie-pop from the time when my brother introduced it to me when he was in third year. I wanted to take music as a subject at school, but it didn't fit in with my options so my parents pay for me to do it outside school. I am learning to play the guitar and the flute.

'Sophie, my best friend, wants me to join the new drama group after school but I don't really want to because it is run by Ms Ryan, my English teacher, who I don't get on with. Sophie is annoyed with me now, especially since we both want to study drama when we leave school. I really don't know what to do. Jean, my other friend, says I'm right not to go because Ms Ryan is a real pain.

'I used to do athletics last year and I came second in the schools' competition. The coach has asked me to start training again because he says we will have a very good relay team if I go along. I said it to my mam and she says it would be a great idea and a good way to keep fit too. Training is on Mondays and Wednesdays after school so it fits in perfectly.

'It is my birthday next week and I'm getting an iPhone. I've saved up the money I got for babysitting and my parents are going to back me the rest. I can't wait because Sophie and all the girls have iPhones already. There's a disco on the night of my birthday too and my parents have said I can go. Some of the lads said they will have some beer and vodka beforehand, but I won't touch it. My mam has told me that you can be arrested for underage drinking so I won't risk that. I'm so looking forward to the disco.'

Individual Activity

Fill in the table opposite by identifying and explaining the people and things that influence the decisions Mandy makes about her life.

	Parents	Friends	Brothers & sisters	Teachers	Celebrities	Media	Law
Hair	Fashion streak				✓		
Clothes						✓	
Make-up		✓					
Diet and exercise				✓		✓	
Hobbies and interests			✓				
Leisure time		✓					
School subjects	✓						
Drinking alcohol							✓
Other							

Pair Activity

1. Who or what has the most influence on Mandy?

   Her friends have the most influence on Mandy because most of the things she does they do

2. Pick one positive influence on Mandy and explain why it is a positive influence.

   The influence of the law because it makes her not want to drink

3. Pick one negative influence on Mandy and explain why it is a negative influence.

   She had dentetion over make-up first because her friends were wearing it

4. Pick one way in which Mandy could have an influence on other people. Give a reason for your choice.

   Mandy wants to do sport. This could influence her friends to do sport

5. Do you think that the influences on Mandy are typical of the influences on teenagers in general? Explain your answer.

   Yes because most teenagers are influenced by these

What are positive and negative influences?

- A positive influence is something that helps you to do the right thing or to achieve your potential.
- A negative influence is something that prevents you from doing your best.

It is important to identify the things that influence the decisions you make because this will help you to understand the choices you make.

As you get older, you become more aware of the people and things that influence you. These include your parents, friends, school, the media and the law. It is important to realise that you also influence other people, including your family, your friends, your class and team mates.

Why do you think it is important to understand how you influence others?

Pair Activity

In pairs, take turns at trying to influence the other person
- The influencer should choose something that they believe the other person should do.
- The other person, has to try and resist the pressure to be influenced.

Examples could be persuading someone to:
- Take up some form of exercise
- Give up smoking
- Take up smoking/drinking
- Buy a product
- Agree to your opinion on an environmental issue
- Mitch class.

Learning *Keepsake*

Three things I have learned about positive and negative influences are:

1. _____
2. _____
3. _____

As a result of what I have learned about positive and negative influences, I will:

_____
_____
_____

_____ has shared this Learning Keepsake with me _____
Name of student   Parent's/guardian's signature

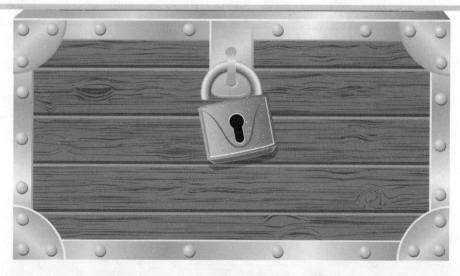

LESSON 17

Body Image

At the end of this lesson . . .
. . . you will understand that there are many different body types and shapes that are normal.

Key Words
- Photoshop
- Body image

Keyskill
- Staying Well
- Managing Information and Thinking

Pair Activity

Look at the covers of well-known magazines or catalogues that are aimed at the teenage market and answer the following questions. Bring in some of your own or look at them online.

1. What messages do the words and the pictures give about body image and beauty?

   The messages the words and pictures give is that you have to be dressed nicely to look good and to be skinny and good looking

2. Do you think the models in the pictures depict typical teenagers? Give reasons for your answer.

   No because the people in these magazines look like they are in they're mid twenties

3. In what ways do the media put pressure on young people to look a certain way?

   The media puts pressure on young people because it makes them feel like they have to look a certain way

4. What effects can these pressures have on ordinary young people?

5. What is considered beautiful in one culture may not be seen as beautiful in another. Name different types of people who are often absent from the media because they are not considered beautiful.

Body types

As you have learned, the media present certain stereotypes of beauty, which are not real. Almost all images used in advertisements and even some images used in films and television programmes have been airbrushed or digitally enhanced. Watch the following clip to see how this is done. The media rarely acknowledge that there are many different body types. They often Photoshop the images they use to make people look taller, thinner or more toned.

Weblink

Watch the video 'Dove Evolution' on YouTube.

Although every person is unique, there are four main body types. Most of us are one of these types.

Rectangle
Body fat is distributed equally. The chest and the hips are roughly the same size. Arms and legs are slender. This body shape can be found in both men and women.

Pear-shaped/triangular
The bottom of your body is larger than the top. A person with a triangle shape typically has narrow shoulders, and a larger bum, legs and thighs.

Apple-shaped
A round body type with more body fat and softer curves. Wide hips, a larger abdomen and shorter legs can also be features of this body type. This body type is common to both men and women.

Hourglass
This shape is found in women only. An hourglass figure is one that has a small waistline with an equal hip and bust line.

Tips for improving your body image

Now that you understand that there are many types of beauty and many different body types, read the following tips on how to improve your body image. Add any of your own tips that are not included.

Individual Activity

1. Identify your body type.
2. Concentrate on the good things about yourself.
3. Wear clothes that complement your good points.
4. Stay fit and healthy by eating a healthy diet and taking regular exercise.
5. Spend time with people who are positive and supportive and who make you feel good about yourself.

Give yourself a makeover

There are certain features of our bodies that we can change. It is important to identify these and, if necessary, to go about changing them in a healthy and safe way. From the list below, choose three elements a person could change to improve their body image. Say why changing these three things would work.

- height
- hair
- eyes
- bone structure

- weight
- posture
- ears
- teeth

- muscle
- size
- feet
- complexion

- mouth
- nose
- level of fitness
- hands

What can you change?

1. Hair
2. Weight
3. Posture

How could changing these things improve your body image?

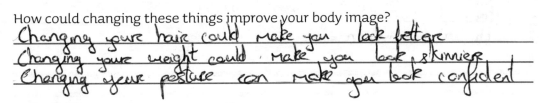

Changing youre hair could make you look better
Changing youre weight could make you look skinnier
Changing youre posture can make you look confident

Weblink

www.bodywhys.ie

Learning *Keepsake*

Three things I have learned about body image are:

1. How to change it
2. How to improve it
3. The things I can and can't change

As a result of what I have learned about body image, I will:

Try to think of myself positively

_____ Conor Kelly _____ has shared this Learning Keepsake with me _____

Name of student   Parent's/guardian's signature

Topic Review

Date / /

In this topic I learned about

Body image

This topic is useful to me in my life because

I now know what I can and can't change

In this topic I liked

The different

In this topic I did not like

I would like to find out more about

How I can change my body image

Key Skills I have used in this topic are:

☑ Managing myself ☐ Being creative

☐ Staying well ☐ Working with others

☐ Communicating ☐ Managing information and thinking

*Are you up for the challenge?

Design a questionnaire on student views of their body image. Carry out the survey and present your findings.

Sexuality and Sexual Health

- Lesson 18 From Conception to Birth

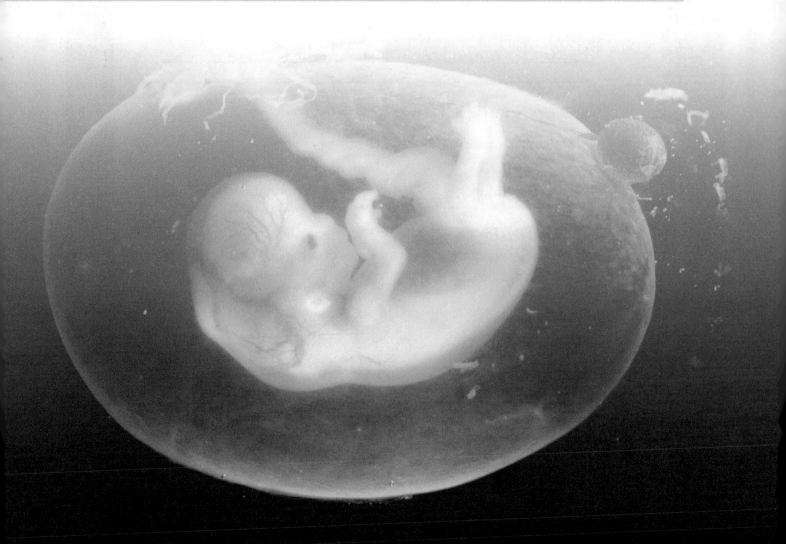

LESSON 18

From Conception to Birth

At the end of this lesson . . .

. . . you will know the stages of development from conception to birth.

Key Words
- Conception
- Foetus
- Contractions
- Dilated

Keyskill
- Staying Well

A healthy pregnancy

Pair Activity

Complete the following cloze test and answer the questions that follow.

> legumes vegetables **HIV** folic acid
>
> spina bifida
>
> shellfish **medication** exercise regime
>
> **raw eggs** alcohol **unpasteurised**
>
> diet reduce birth weight tobacco

A woman planning a baby should have a healthy _____ _____ and _____. It is important to take _____ before and during pregnancy. This has been shown to reduce the risk of _____ _____ . Sources include leafy _____ and _____ . Pregnant women should avoid _____ and _____ during pregnancy. Drinking can affect the development of the baby and smoking during pregnancy can cause low _____ _____. A pregnant woman should consult her GP before taking _____. During pregnancy certain foods should be avoided: _____ dairy products, _____ and _____ could cause food poisoning and harm the unborn child. All pregnant women are routinely tested for _____ . This is because if the test is positive certain drugs can be given to the mother to_____ the chances of the baby contracting the virus.

Individual Activity

1. Write down three things a woman could do to prepare for pregnancy.
   a) _____
   b) _____
   c) _____

2. Why do you think it is important for a woman to take care of her body when she is planning a pregnancy?
   _____
   _____
   _____

3. List three people who could support a pregnant woman and suggest what kind of support they could offer.

a) _____

b) _____

c) _____

From conception to birth

Conception to week 4

After the woman's egg has been fertilised by the man's sperm it forms a single cell. This cell first divides into two, then into four, then into eight and so on. The ball of cells moves along the Fallopian tube to the womb. Once in the womb it divides into the embryo and placenta and embeds itself in the lining of the womb.

Environment

For the duration of the pregnancy the baby lives inside the uterus (womb).
The baby is protected in a fluid-filled sac called the amniotic sac. The fluid in the amniotic sac is released during childbirth: this is what happens when the waters break.

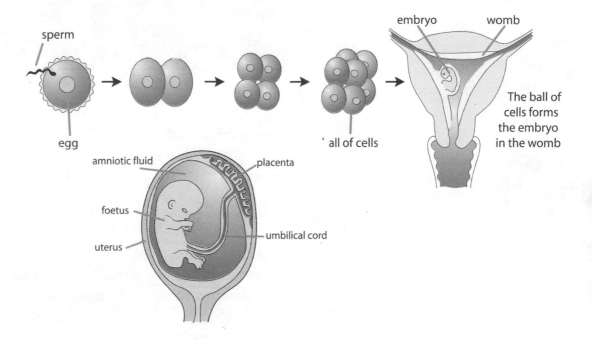

Stages of development

Weeks 5–8

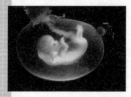

At this stage the baby is referred to as a foetus rather than an embryo. All the baby's organs are in place and continue to develop. The face is forming, and if the mother were to have an ultrasound now, she would be able to hear the baby's heart beat.

The arms and legs appear as buds. The baby is about the size of a five cent coin.

Weeks 8–12

In weeks 9 and 10 the facial features form. The baby is fully formed by week 12 and will continue to grow for the rest of the pregnancy. The placenta is fully developed, passing oxygen and nutrients from the mother to the baby and carrying away carbon dioxide and waste via the umbilical cord.

Weeks 12–20

The baby continues to grow. Movement may be felt by weeks 16–18. By week 18 the eyelashes and eyebrows begin to grow. By week 20 the foetus is now about 11cm long and its sex can be identified by ultrasound.

Weeks 20–40

By week 28 the baby has reached a weight and stage of organ development that would enable it to survive outside the womb with some support; the baby would need help with breathing and feeding until it became more mature. By week 36 the baby is more restricted in the uterus and the head settles downwards in preparation for birth.

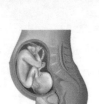

In the last three weeks the pregnancy reaches full term and the baby can be born at any time now. The baby lies head down waiting for the birth.

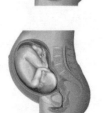

The three stages of birth

There are 3 stages of birth:

1. **From the start of contractions to fully dilated.**
- When the baby is ready to be born the mother experiences painful contractions.
- The contractions cause the neck of the womb to open. This stage of the birth is called labour.
- When the neck of the womb (called the cervix) is fully dilated – ten centimetres wide – the baby is ready to be born.
- The waters can break at any time during the birth.
- There are several different strategies to help the mother through labour pains. These include breathing/relaxation techniques, painkilling injections, epidurals, and Entonox (gas and air).

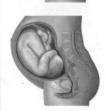

2. **From fully dilated to delivery of the baby.**
- The baby moves through the birth canal (vagina), aided by the mother's pushing and the powerful contractions.
- When the widest part of the baby's head is delivered, this is known as crowning.
- Once the baby is delivered the umbilical cord is clamped and cut.
- The baby's first cry enables the lungs to inflate with air.

3. **Delivery of the placenta.**
- After the baby is born, the placenta dislodges itself from the lining of the womb and is expelled by contractions.
- The mother sometimes receives an injection after the baby is born to aid this process.

Caesarean section

Caesarean section is when the baby is delivered by cutting the womb through the lower abdomen. This method is performed if there are complications in pregnancy or childbirth, for example in a breech birth, if the baby is distressed, or if the cervix does not dilate fully.

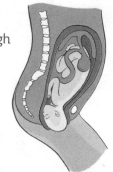

Crossword: conception to birth

Across

8 This connects the embryo to the placenta and later forms the baby's bellybutton.
9 Food and oxygen pass from the mother to the baby through this.
10 This occurs when the widest part of the baby's head is delivered.
11 These occur when the baby is ready to be born.
12 The joining together of the female's egg and the male's sperm.

Down

1 .... dairy products should be avoided during pregnancy.
2 You should take this if you are planning to have a baby.
3 The egg is located here when it is ready to be fertilised.
4 This fluid protects the baby and prevents it from being injured.
5 A normal pregnancy lasts about ...... months.
6 This waste substance passes from the baby to the mother.
7 The baby lives here for the duration of the pregnancy.

Learning *Keepsake*

Three things I have learned about conception and birth are:

1. _____
2. _____
3. _____

As a result of what I have learned about conception and birth, I will:

_____
_____
_____

_____ has shared this Learning Keepsake with me _____

Name of student   Parent's/guardian's signature

Topic Review

Date / /

In this topic I learned about

_____

This topic is useful to me in my life because

_____

_____

In this topic I liked

_____

_____

In this topic I did not like

_____

_____

I would like to find out more about

_____

_____

Key Skills I have used in this topic are:

☐ Managing myself
☐ Staying well
☐ Communicating
☐ Being creative
☐ Working with others
☐ Managing information and thinking

*Are you up for the challenge?
Create a leaflet giving information and advice for an expectant mother.

TOPIC 9

Relationship Spectrum

● Lesson 19 Peer Pressure and Other Influences

LESSON 19

Peer Pressure and Other Influences

At the end of this lesson . . .
. . . you will have analysed how young people are influenced by their friends
. . . you will have identified strategies for dealing with peer pressure.

Key Words
- Peers
- Pressure
- Authority

Keyskill
- Working with Others

Who influences us?

Sometimes it is hard to identify who has influence over us. Many studies suggest that young people are most influenced by their family and their close friends.
However, it can also be argued that peer pressure has a big impact on the behaviour of young people. Peers are people of similar age to you who share the same experiences and interests as you. Peer pressure can be positive or negative.

Group Activity

Below are some examples of positive and negative peer pressure.

Positive	Negative
You and your friends meet up once a week to study	Your friend wants you to watch sexual material on the internet and you don't want to

Individual Activity

Now that you have identified some positive and negative examples of peer pressure, answer the following questions by ticking the appropriate box.

1. You go along with your friends even if you do not agree with what they are doing.
   Like me ☐   Not like me ☐

2. It is important for you that you do not stand out from your peers.
   Like me ☐   Not like me ☐

3. You would go along with your friends just so that you do not lose face.
   Like me ☐   Not like me ☐

4. You feel embarrassed if you are not allowed do what your friends are doing.
   Like me ☐   Not like me ☐

5. At times, you find it difficult to stand up for what you believe in.
   Like me ☐   Not like me ☐

Teenagers and peer pressure

If you found that you are quite affected by peer pressure, you are not alone. Teenagers are probably the people who are most influenced by peer pressure. Standing up to peer pressure can be difficult. Most people want to fit in and to be liked and it is easier to go along with the crowd so as not to be left out. Peer pressure to dress a certain way is one thing, but going along with the crowd to drink and smoke is another. In other words, some forms of peer pressure can be dangerous and get us into trouble.

Tips on resisting peer pressure

- Remember, it is your life: you do not have to give excuses or apologies for what you believe in.
- Take time to decide what you want to say and do; and stick with your decision.
- Do not be persuaded by others trying to make you feel guilty by saying things like 'If you were any fun you would do it.'
- Do not fight back or make accusations.
- A true friend will respect your decision. They will not fall out with you simply because you do not want to do something.
- If the pressure does not stop, walk away.

Class Activity

Weblink

Go to www.b4udecide.ie

Read the following case study and discuss the questions that follow.

Case Study

Pamela has been going out with John for a couple of months. Katie is a very good friend of Pamela's but lately she feels like a bit of a gooseberry. Pamela is constantly trying to set Katie up with John's friend Kevin. Katie has met Kevin and likes him, but she does not feel ready to start dating him. Pamela has told Katie that the next time they meet up she will leave them on their own together. Katie does not want that.

Individual Activity

1. Do you think Pamela is being fair to her friend?
2. Should Katie meet Kevin and just see what happens?
3. Why do you think people try to pressurise other people into making decisions?
4. Give examples of other types of peer pressure young people experience surrounding relationships.

Learning *Keepsake*

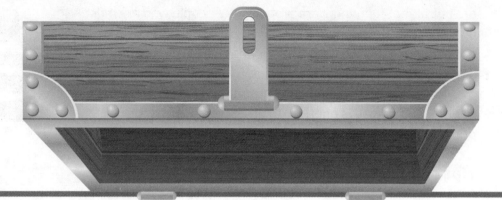

Three things I have learned about peer pressure and other influences are:

1. _____
2. _____
3. _____

As a result of what I have learned about peer pressure and other influences, I will:

_____
_____
_____

_____ has shared this Learning Keepsake with me _____

Name of student   Parent's/guardian's signature

Topic Review

Date / /

In this topic I learned about

_____

This topic is useful to me in my life because

_____

_____

In this topic I liked

_____

_____

In this topic I did not like

_____

_____

I would like to find out more about

_____

_____

Key Skills I have used in this topic are:

- ☐ Managing myself
- ☐ Staying well
- ☐ Communicating
- ☐ Being creative
- ☐ Working with others
- ☐ Managing information and thinking

*Are you up for the challenge?

Design a wrist band with a symbol on it to remind young people of how to resist peer pressure.

Special Relationships

- Lesson 20 Recognising and Expressing Feelings and Emotions
- Lesson 21 Managing Relationships
- Lesson 22 Health and Personal Safety

LESSON 20

Recognising and Expressing Feelings and Emotions

At the end of this lesson . . .
. . . you will know more about the emotional sides of different relationships

. . . you will have developed skills for communicating in relationships

Key Words
- Appropriate
- Conflict
- Resolution

Keyskill
- Communicating

Learning to get along

When you were a child you were totally dependent on your parents to look after you and make decisions for you.

As you grow older you become more independent and you form relationships with a wide variety of people. You also have more responsibilities and you must consider not just your own feelings but the feelings of others too. At this stage this is all pretty new, so you have to learn to recognise your feelings and express them appropriately.

In every relationship people will have their disagreements. The important thing is that these disagreements do not get out of control. You do not want disagreements to turn into screaming matches where people say hurtful things. Therefore it is necessary for people to discuss their feelings in a way that allows an agreement to be reached.

Pair Activity

1. With the help of your partner, fill in the table below by identifying some of the possible disagreements that might occur between the following people.

A teenager and their family	Friends	Boyfriends/ girlfriends

2. Suggest how each disagreement might be resolved.

A teenager and their family	Friends	Boyfriends/ girlfriends

Tips for conflict resolution

1. Try to sort out the problem as soon as possible.
2. Wait until both you and the other person are calm before you do this.
3. Do not bring up past disagreements.
4. Stick to the facts while saying how you feel.
5. Remain calm and try not to blame or insult the other person.
6. Tell them how the problem is affecting you.
7. Try to reach an agreement that is best for both of you.

Role Play

Choose one of the following scenarios and use the tips for conflict resolution to role play a resolution to the scenario.

Scenario 1

Girl 1: You have fancied a boy in your rowing club for as long as you can remember. Your friend knows that you like him. You have just found out that this boy has asked your friend out. You are meeting your friend tonight.

Girl 2: One of the boys from the rowing club has asked you out. You think he is really nice, but you know that your friend likes him a lot.

Scenario 2

Boy: You have been going steady with your girlfriend. Although you really like her, at the disco on Saturday night you kissed another girl in your class. You don't think anyone saw you. You are meeting your girlfriend tonight.

Girl: You have been going steady with your boyfriend. You couldn't go to the disco with him on Saturday night because you were babysitting. You heard he kissed another girl and you are meeting him tonight.

Learning *Keepsake*

Three things I have learned about expressing feelings and emotions are:

1. _____
2. _____
3. _____

As a result of what I have learned about expressing feelings and emotions, I will:

_____
_____

_____ has shared this Learning Keepsake with me _____
Name of student   Parent's/guardian's signature

LESSON 21

Managing Relationships

At the end of this lesson . . .

. . . you will have examined some of things that influence young people when starting boyfriend/girlfriend relationships

. . . and you will have identified ways of managing relationships.

Key Words
- Advantages
- Disadvantages
- Relationships

 # Keyskill
- Communicating

Individual Activity

Discuss the following questions and write down the answers you come up with.

1. What pressures are young people under surrounding relationships or sexuality?

   _____

   _____

   _____

2. What age do you think a person should be before they have their first boyfriend or girlfriend? Give reasons for your answer.

   _____

   _____

   _____

3. Are there different expectations in relationships for boys and girls?

   _____

   _____

   _____

4. What messages do young people receive about relationships/sexuality from media industry?

   _____

   _____

   _____

Individual Activity

Discuss your answers as a class.

Managing relationships: boyfriend/girlfriend relationships

When you are ready to start a relationship with a boy or a girl, it is very important that you do so for the right reasons. Just because some of your friends are in a relationship does not meant that you have to follow suit. There may be other things in your life that are far more important to you at the moment, for example friends, sport or study. Just because you are not interested in anyone at the moment does not mean you won't be in the future. Your time will come.

Individual Activity

When you are ready to be in a relationship it is very important to be able to recognise the qualities that make a good relationship. Look at the qualities listed below and say why they are important for a good relationship. List any other qualities you also think are important for a good relationship and say why.

1. Honesty is important for a good relationship because

2. Loyalty is important for a good relationship because

3. Empathy is important for a good relationship because

4. Respect is important for a good relationship because

5. Generosity is important for a good relationship because

Weblink

Go to www.b4udecide.ie and watch the video 'Dealing with Peer Pressure'

Learning *Keepsake*

Three things I have learned about managing relationships are:

1. _____
2. _____
3. _____

As a result of what I have learned about managing relationships, I will:

_____
_____
_____

_____ has shared this Learning Keepsake with me _____

Name of student   Parent's/guardian's signature

LESSON 22

Health and Personal Safety

At the end of this lesson . . .
. . . you will be aware of the importance of staying safe in forming new relationships.

Key Words
- Personal
- Safety
- Expectations

Keyskill
- Staying Safe

Before the disco . . .

During the disco . . .

After the disco . . .

Class Activity

1. Do young people dress a certain way when they are going to discos or parties?
2. Do you think it is easier for boys or girls to get ready for a disco or party?
3. What expectations are there on young people to score, kiss or meet at discos?
4. Are there different pressures for boys and girls to behave a certain way at a disco or in a relationship?
5. How can you ensure that you stay safe when you are out with your friends?
6. If you met someone you like at a disco, how would you contact them again?
7. What safety issues do you need to consider when starting a new relationship with a boyfriend or girlfriend?

Staying healthy and safe

Meeting new people can be exciting. When you are young there are loads of new opportunities to do this. Over the next few years you might even have your first boyfriend or girlfriend. If you are not yet interested in having a boyfriend or girlfriend, don't worry: people develop at different stages, and you will know when you are ready. It is important not to be pressurised into anything you are not ready for. There can be certain expectations on young people to conform and to behave in certain ways. If you go to a disco, for example, there may be pressure to score, or to kiss another person just for the sake of it. Just remember: it is okay to be yourself and to behave the way that you think is appropriate.

Pair Activity

In pairs come up with ways people can stay safe at parties and discos.

Learning *Keepsake*

Three things I have learned about personal safety are:

1. _____
2. _____
3. _____

As a result of what I have learned about personal safety, I will:

_____
_____
_____

_____ has shared this Learning Keepsake with me _____

Name of student   Parent's/guardian's signature

Topic Review

Date / /

In this topic I learned about

_____

This topic is useful to me in my life because

_____

_____

In this topic I liked

_____

_____

In this topic I did not like

_____

_____

I would like to find out more about

_____

_____

Key Skills I have used in this topic are:

☐ Managing myself
☐ Staying well
☐ Communicating
☐ Being creative
☐ Working with others
☐ Managing information and thinking

*Are you up for the challenge?
As a class, organise a 'Respect for All' week.

Substance Use

- Lesson 23 The Effects of Drugs
- Lesson 24 Alcohol and its Effects: Why/Why Not?
- Lesson 25 Cannabis and its Effects: Why/Why Not?

LESSON 23

The Effects of Drugs

At the end of this lesson . . .

. . . you will have reviewed the physical and psychological effects of drugs.

Key Words
- Dependence
- Psychological

Keyskill
- Staying Safe

What are drugs?

A drug is defined as a chemical that changes the way the human body functions – mentally, physically or emotionally.

Drugs may be:
- useful or harmful
- socially acceptable or socially unacceptable
- addictive or non-addictive
- legal or illegal.

The definition above includes many substances we naturally think of as drugs (e.g. alcohol, solvents, tobacco) as well as substances we don't often normally consider to be drugs (e.g. coffee, tea).

Name that drug

Complete the crossword to help you identify different types of drug. You'll find the answers among the words in the box on the next page.

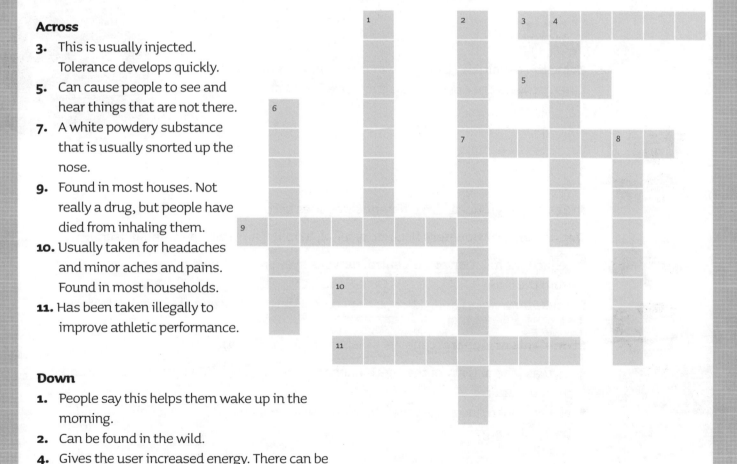

Across

3. This is usually injected. Tolerance develops quickly.
5. Can cause people to see and hear things that are not there.
7. A white powdery substance that is usually snorted up the nose.
9. Found in most houses. Not really a drug, but people have died from inhaling them.
10. Usually taken for headaches and minor aches and pains. Found in most households.
11. Has been taken illegally to improve athletic performance.

Down

1. People say this helps them wake up in the morning.
2. Can be found in the wild.
4. Gives the user increased energy. There can be other substances mixed in with it.
6. Found in inhalers used by asthmatics.
8. Many young people try this drug and then find it incredibly hard to give up.

Words

nicotine **caffeine** cannabis steroids

ecstasy solvents

magic mushrooms **aspirin** Ventolin

cocaine **alcohol** LSD

heroin **tranquillisers**

Drug misuse

Drug misuse is the use of any drug, legal or illegal, that damages some aspect of the user's life, whether it is their mental or physical health, their relationship with their family, friends or society in general.

Class Activity

Using the definition above and what you know, brainstorm the different ways drug misuse can damage aspects of:

1. a person's life
2. a person's family life
3. society.

Drugs can be grouped into different categories according to their effects.

Depressants or downers (include alcohol, heroin, cannabis and tranquillisers):

- reduce the function of the central nervous system, slowing down messages to and from the brain
- cause drowsiness, relaxation, lack of co-ordination, concentration and judgement.

Stimulants or uppers (caffeine, amphetamines, ecstasy):

- increase the activity of the central nervous system, speeding up messages to and from the brain
- elevate mood, increase wakefulness and give an increased sense of mental and physical energy.

Hallucinogens (LSD, ecstasy, cannabis, magic mushrooms):

- distort the way people see or hear things
- cause lack of contact with reality.

Opiates (morphine, codeine, methadone, heroin):

- are strong painkillers
- produce feelings of euphoria and sleeplessness.

Drug dependence

There are two types of dependence: physical and psychological.

- **Physical** dependence occurs when the body needs the drug to function normally. Absence of the drug causes withdrawal symptoms such as nausea, vomiting, sweating, tremors and delirium, muscular cramps and constipation.
- **Psychological** dependence occurs when the person feels they need the drug to be happy, to feel normal and to cope with life. This can be more difficult to overcome than physical dependence.

Tolerance occurs when the body gets used to a drug and needs larger amounts to achieve the same effects.

Individual Activity

Using what you have learned in this lesson, list as many drugs as you can think of under each heading in the table. (Some drugs may fit into more than one category.)

Useful	Harmful	Socially acceptable	Socially unacceptable	Addictive	Non-addictive	Legal	Illegal

Learning *Keepsake*

Three things I have learned about the effects of drugs are:

1. _____

2. _____

3. _____

As a result of what I have learned about the effects of drugs, I will:

_____

_____

_____

_____ has shared this Learning Keepsake with me _____

Name of student   Parent/guardian's signature

LESSON 24

Alcohol and its Effects: Why/ Why Not?

At the end of this lesson . . .
. . . you will know more about the effects of alcohol
. . . and you will be able to make more informed decisions about using alcohol.

Key Words
- Alcohol
- Depressant
- Side effects

Keyskill
- Managing Myself
- Staying Safe

Faced with the sober reality of a drunken night out with our teens

As the commuters queued for the buses to go home, the teenagers began to queue to get into the nightclubs around town. At half past six on a busy city street, the barriers went up outside one of the clubs to keep order among the youngsters who were celebrating the results of their Junior Cert.

First in line are the boys, with their spiked-up hair and pastel-coloured T-shirts, then they are joined by their girlfriends, who are whooping and shouting with joy at the results they received earlier on in the day. After a few minutes, a small boy, who looks no more than eleven, joins them. He hugs all the girls in the group, who are twice the height of him, his ginger hair and freckles giving him the appearance of one of their younger brothers. But then one of them announces: 'You'd better sober up, Micko, or they won't let you in.'

One of the T-shirt-clad boys urinates against the newsagents' wall, while another young boy slowly grinds against his girlfriend as he leans her back against his chest, waiting for the nightclub to open. Yet another teen takes a long sip out of his can of Dutch Gold, oblivious to the bouncers on the door.

Later, across town, where a non-alcoholic disco is well under way, there is a controlled atmosphere as the Gardaí maintain a presence around the disco. Around 50 teenage boys squeeze their heads through the closed gates like caged animals in the zoo, desperately trying to get in to see the mini-skirted young girls who wait for them on the inside. The disco is full and the bouncers are no longer letting anyone else in. Demand for the event is so strong that tickets have actually been forged for it. One of the bouncers displays his find; they look so close to the real thing that it's almost impossible to tell the difference. It's a story that we have become accustomed to in the last few years: teenagers are hanging out in non-alcoholic discos, but they're going into them inebriated.

While we should never become immune to the sight of a drunken teenager, it's a sad fact that it simply isn't that shocking any more. We shrug our shoulders and say to each other that it wasn't like that in our day. However, when I was faced with the cold reality of what can happen, it's not so easy to adopt such a blasé attitude.

At 9pm, the time when most people are just setting out on their night out, the Junior Cert celebrations are already in full swing on another central street. I come across two young girls sitting on the steps near the bus station. Originally I intended to ask them how they had done in their exams and how they were celebrating, but after the first few seconds it was clear that this didn't matter to either of them. One of them is sitting with her head lolling from side to side as her white Wonderbra pokes out of her top. Her skirt is hitched around her waist as she starts to cry. Her friend, who is sober, is fighting back the tears as the second girl apologises.

I had come across the two girls mid-debate over a ruined night, one too drunk to move, too drunk to think, too drunk to protect herself. The drunk girl wants to stay around for another two hours. 'How long does it take to sober up?' she asks me pleadingly. She tells me that she had been drinking gin and vodka. Her friend adds that sometimes this had been with Coke, sometimes straight. She hadn't been allowed into the nightclub because she was too drunk and her sober friend had drawn the short straw by staying with her.

A few hundred yards away, the rest of their friends are partying away in the basement of a hotel, oblivious as the two young girls sit on the steps. The drunk girl had gone out to celebrate getting five As and four Bs in her Junior Cert. She was promised an iPod if she did well but now, coming home in this state, she isn't sure if she's going to get it. This was the first time she had been drinking, she tells me.

As I try to persuade the girls to ring one of their mothers, a young man, a few years older, sits down on the step beside them. 'I have a boyfriend,' one of them immediately objects, but this man doesn't care. Seeing two young girls on the steps, one with her shoes thrown off, skirt hitched high and ladders in her tights, he sees an opportunity to pounce and he takes it. 'I'm not going anywhere,' he says, as he becomes increasingly aggressive. A group of his friends stroll by, but he remains, with no interest in what the rest of his friends are doing, just in trying to sidle up to the girls. Then he offers the drunk girl some 'water' he was holding in a Volvic bottle. In her drunken state, she reaches out to take it until I intervene. Increasingly annoyed that his plans were being foiled, he stands up and delivers a barrage of abuse before eventually moving on.

There is no one else on the streets, no one who could have helped them. As soon as he leaves, the girl begins to vomit, the clear liquid pouring out of her lipstick-smudged mouth. Her mascara starts to run, leaving black tear marks on her face. 'I'm so sorry,' she repeats over and over to her friend. 'I'm sorry I ruined your night. Please don't ring my mum. Wait with me until twelve.'

Eventually, we ring her mother, who fortunately is just a ten-minute drive away. She pulls her car in across the road, marches over and hoists her daughter off the ground. Trying to stand up, she slips in her own vomit.

The friend is left on her own, her friends don't have their phones, she tells me. I bring her down to the nightclub where her friends are, only to find the doors are shut. After I persuade one of the bouncers to let my 'little sister' in, she thankfully rejoins them. Meanwhile, her friend is on the drive home with her mother, who barely even acknowledged my presence as a stranger, assisting her daughter. And the only apology she made was to the friend whose night was ruined. Perhaps she didn't realise that it could have been not just two little girls' nights, but their lives, that were ruined that night.

Source: Sunday Independent, 18 September 2007

Individual Activity

1. Do you think this story is realistic?

_____

2. In what ways are the two girls putting their personal safety at risk?

_____

_____

_____

3. In what ways are the males in the story putting their safety at risk?

_____

_____

_____

3. Using the information in the story as a prompt, make a list of all of the effects of drinking to excess.

The effects of alcohol

1. Using alcohol while you are still developing causes brain damage.

During adolescence the brain is still developing. Drinking during this time can lead to long-term irreversible damage, including memory loss.

2. Drinking alcohol can lead to obesity.

Alcohol is high in calories. One standard drink can contain over 200 calories. Drinking alcohol can also create a false appetite and contribute to a bad diet, for example eating fast food that is high in fat and low in nutrients after a night out.

3. Starting to drink during adolescence increases the risk of becoming dependent on alcohol in later life.

Evidence shows that the way the adolescent brain develops means that young people who start drinking in their early teens are more likely to become addicted.

4. Alcohol can cause depression.

Because alcohol appears to give a person high or increased energy, it can be mistaken for a stimulant. But it is actually a depressant. If a young person drinks alcohol they may notice a drop in their mood over the following days. This can be unpleasant.

5. Drinking too much alcohol can lead to alcohol poisoning, which can cause death.

It takes the body one hour to break down one standard drink. Strong coffee, cold showers or fresh air will not help a person sober up: only time will remove alcohol from the system. Drinking on a full stomach will delay the absorption of alcohol into the bloodstream, but it will not prevent you getting drunk.

6. Alcohol increases the risk of road accidents.
Over 100 people die due to alcohol-related crashes every year. Even after only one drink, a driver is three times more likely to be involved in a crash.

Individual Activity

Fill in the table below.

How I feel about alcohol	Agree	Disagree	Don't know
The drinking age limit should be reduced			
Getting drunk is stupid – you just make a fool of yourself			
Young people drink because there is nothing else to do			
Learning about the effects of alcohol is pointless – young people will drink no matter what they are told			
Having friends who drink means you are more likely to drink			
Alcohol helps people cope with their problems			
You're not harming anyone by underage drinking			
I'll wait until the legal age before I drink			

Learning *Keepsake*

Three things I have learned about alcohol are:

1. _____

2. _____

3. _____

As a result of what I have learned about alcohol, I will:

_____

_____

_____

_____ has shared this Learning Keepsake with me _____

Name of student   Parent's/guardian's signature

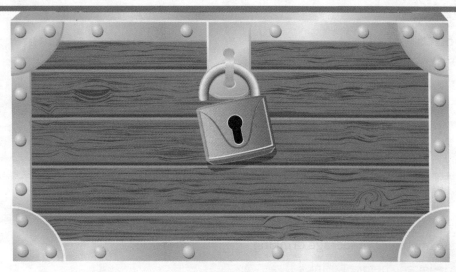

LESSON 25

Cannabis and its Effects: Why/ Why Not?

At the end of this lesson . . .
. . . you will be aware of the health, social and legal implications of using cannabis
. . . and you will be able to identify reasons why cannabis should be avoided.

Key Words
- Cannabis
- Depressant
- Dependence

Keyskill
- Staying Well
- Managing Myself

Pair Activity

What do you know about cannabis?

Complete the following true or false quiz to determine how much you know about cannabis.

Statement	True	False	Unsure
Cannabis is not like other drugs – it is completely safe to take because it is naturally grown			
Smoking cannabis is not as bad for your health as smoking cigarettes			
Cannabis is the most widely used illegal drug in Ireland			
If you use cannabis you are not really doing anything wrong			
Cannabis can be detected in a person's body for up to 30 days after use			
Gardaí have no way of knowing if a driver has used cannabis			
You can't become addicted to cannabis			
Cannabis use only has pleasant effects			
It is illegal to grow, produce, supply or possess cannabis for medical or non-medical use			
A person with a drug conviction will be refused a visa for the USA			

What is cannabis?

Cannabis is naturally occurring – it is made from the cannabis plant. The potency of cannabis is usually expressed in terms of its THC content. THC (tetrahydrocannabinol) is the ingredient in cannabis responsible for it euphoric effect.

Cannabis users can experience mood-altering effects. The precise effects of cannabis on a person can depend on a number of factors, including:

- the strength of the cannabis
- the length of time it has been stored
- the amount that has been used
- the way it is taken
- the experience, mood and expectations of the user.

Different types of cannabis

Although it's all from the same plant, cannabis comes in many different forms. Drug products made from the cannabis plant vary enormously in their THC content. The three types are cannabis resin, herbal cannabis and cannabis oil.

Cannabis resin

This is frequently referred to as hash. Hash, which is made from the resin of the cannabis plant, is a soft black or brown lump that looks rather like an Oxo cube. It is scraped down to a powder for use.

Herbal cannabis

Commonly known as grass, marijuana, pot, weed or (in its stronger form) skunk, herbal cannabis looks like dried herbs.

Cannabis oil

Also referred to as hash oil, this is the least common and the most powerful form of cannabis.

How is cannabis taken?

People take cannabis in a few different ways:

- mixed with tobacco and rolled in a homemade cigarette known as a spliff or a joint
- smoked using a pipe called a bong
- mixed into drinks or baked into cakes or cookies. Taken this way, the effects of cannabis can be more difficult to predict or to control.

What are the effects of using cannabis?

Short-term effects

- Increased heart rate and lowered blood pressure.
- Interferes with short-term memory and learning abilities. Even simple arithmetic skills can be disrupted for 24 hours after a high.
- Increased appetite – this is sometimes called the 'munchies'.
- Inability to perform complex tasks such as driving or using machinery.
- It may cause feelings of anxiety, suspicion, confusion, panic and paranoia.

Long-term effects

- Regular cannabis use can lead to an increased risk of the mental illness schizophrenia in vulnerable people.
- Cannabis use can result in fertility problems for both men and women.
- The smoke and tar from a joint impairs lung function.
- Regular users of cannabis may experience lack of motivation or ambition. Research shows that regular cannabis use increases the likelihood of the user dropping out of school.
- Cannabis can affect the way the brain works. Regular, heavy use makes it difficult to learn and concentrate. Heavy users perform poorly in exams.
- It can put pressure on the heart, thus increasing the heart rate, and affect blood pressure, which can be especially harmful for those with heart disease.
- Smoking while pregnant may increase the risk of the baby being born smaller than expected.

Most young teenagers have no interest in taking drugs. Sometimes people take drugs because an opportunity arises. People may feel awkward, pressurised or embarrassed about saying no.

Pair Activity

Prepare a short role play for the following scenario. Take turns at refusing the joint. Use some of the assertiveness skills you learned in Lesson 7 to help you.

Have a Go

Your friend's parents are away, so she has asked you and a few other friends from school to call over. While you are there one of the boys starts to roll a joint. You know that the joint is going to be passed around.

Learning *Keepsake*

Three things I have learned about cannabis are:

1. _____
2. _____
3. _____

As a result of what I have learned about cannabis, I will:

_____
_____
_____

_____ has shared this Learning Keepsake with me _____

Name of student   Parent's/guardian's signature

Topic Review

Date / /

In this topic I learned about

_____

This topic is useful to me in my life because

_____

_____

In this topic I liked

_____

_____

In this topic I did not like

_____

_____

I would like to find out more about

_____

_____

Key Skills I have used in this topic are:

- ☐ Managing myself
- ☐ Staying well
- ☐ Communicating
- ☐ Being creative
- ☐ Working with others
- ☐ Managing information and thinking

*Are you up for the challenge?

Design a media campaign about the consequences of alcohol use and where and how to get help for alcohol related problems.